ACTIVATE YOUR GALACTIC 12 STRAND DNA

CHANNELED TRANSMISSIONS FROM ANGELS RAPHAEL AND ARIEL

NEW EARTH SERIES PART 2

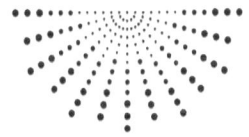

ADRIA ESTRIBOU

Wing**Sound**Media

Activate Your Galactic 12 Strand DNA:

Channeled Transmissions from Angels Raphael and Ariel

New Earth Series Part 2

Adria Estribou

First Edition 2025. Published in the United States.

Published by Wing Sound Media

www.WingSound.com

P.O. Box 3401

Sedona, AZ 86340

info@wingsoundmedia.com

Paperback

ISBN: 978-1-967025-05-3

My profound thanks to those who over the years (and in this book!) have asked the deep questions that prompted and nourished insights coming through from Angels Raphael and Ariel.

Thank you for sharing this path of learning and exploration with me and the angels.

CONTENTS

PREFACE

I didn't intend to be a channel. The process of being a conscious channel for beings looking to support humanity's evolution has often been surprising. This book, I have to say, came as a shock.

When I started channeling angels Raphael and Ariel publicly in 2018, they spoke about the sea change happening for humanity—the emergence of what many call New Earth. Part 1 in this series focused on some of the big themes of change, including freedom, moving from third to fifth dimension, the end of contracts and destiny, and creating your life through heart wishes.

This topic for this book wasn't on my radar at all. Typically, the angels give a title of an upcoming transmission and sometimes a sentence or two of description. I really don't know what to expect from the channeling session in advance. Sometimes it is a lecture-style information topic, sometimes energetic exercises or meditations. I experience it along with everyone else.

This book was channeled from March through August 2025 in Sedona, Arizona in a series of weekly live online group transmissions.

It all started with a transmission they had given the title "Interdimensional Wish Fields." I had no idea becoming a 12-dimensional human would be the topic, or that they would channel for six months straight on the same theme (they had not done this before).

The overall theme is how we as humans are profoundly shifting from *Homo sapiens* into something new—a "New Human" with 12 galactic strands of DNA.

Why these 12? Why giant and not unicorn? Why Sirian but not Orion? My understanding is that these 12 galactic types of beings joined together to form humankind. So it is not a commentary about these being the twelve best races; it's more of a historical fact. These are our forebears in a genetic sense.

In addition to that, you may be a starseed from another galactic race. Or you may have soul memories of being on another planet. The activation of these 12 galactic DNA strands in us now does not discount any of that.

You still have your individual memories, missions and leanings (things you like best). You don't lose that, the same way sharing common traits with *Homo sapiens* didn't make you any less unique as an individual human.

What I appreciate about the angels' approach is they give context but also practical guidance with how to feel into and play into what we are now, and what this opens up for us. They are not going to tell you what to do with these new abilities and perspectives.

That, dear friends, is up to us!

If you are reading this now, you are a pioneer. I hope you enjoy the empowerment and adventure that activating these 12 dimensional lines opens up for you.

With love, Adria

A NOTE ABOUT READING TRANSMISSIONS

These are activations, not just words. When you are reading the words, please take the time to absorb, integrate, or be in reflection or meditation. Pause as needed. There is a lot of energy coming through, not just information.

For the longer meditations and energy exercises in the book, links to free online recordings are provided. The audio is from the live transmissions. Quiet spaces without channeled words in meditations were left in the recording on purpose so that you can sink deep into the meditation.

Please don't drive while you listen. Activations/meditations work best when your focus isn't needed on other tasks—such as caring for a small child or operating equipment—for safety and also for you to fully receive.

1

GALACTIC DNA

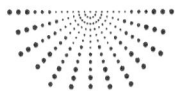

This is Angel Raphael. Much of your wishing to date has been about the circumstances and the people in the dimensions that you are in. And sometimes it's been about encountering galactic friends or interdimensional travel, but still from the vantage point of where you are—we could say some bifurcation of third and fifth dimension. Most of you reading this are pretty fully in fifth by this date. What does that mean for the other aspects of you that are overlaid in other dimensions?

We'll speak about this today, in terms of your developmental wishing, and your development into other parts of you. Travel was the first way that we encountered the other dimensions by leaning in through the senses or the heart, looking in or looking out, to begin to explore and experience what are the flavors, the touch, the sounds, the sights of other dimensions?*

And you will get more adept at that as time goes on and the physical self becomes more and more able to sustain that, which means that

---

* English-language course on interdimensional travel available online at www.adriaestribou.love/shop

1

gives your senses, inner and outer senses time to catch up, to piece together more resiliently "what is the picture? What's really going on in these other dimensions?" so that you can interact more fully there. We are aware that that's the beginning, for most of you, that journey—interdimensional travel. At the same time, you are aware that you have other aspects of yourself in the dream space, in meditation, that seem to go elsewhere or experience other things than your physical and energetic self that experiences what's happening right here right now. That's what we are going to speak about more today. What happens as you become more interdimensional—you yourself as a being—and how does that impact what you may want to wish for and grow into?

It's a big topic, but we will begin this now. The overview here is that you are and have been human, but we've been speaking about the cellular changes to you as a human self now expanding in certain ways. We've been speaking in concrete terms about gifts and abilities, and we've been speaking about solar light shifting the cellular structure of you. But what does that mean in terms of multi dimensionality? It means that the old human was essentially calibrated for third dimension, and you've stretched it a bit to take it over into fourth and other dimensions, and then the new human started to come online, and new human is most comfortable as a baseline in fifth or fourth, sometimes so very heart centered in the practical world, more in fourth and fifth as the baseline benchmark. But as more of you come, so to speak, online, some of those aspects are more comfortable in other dimensions.

Each of you has, for example, a strand of galactic DNA being activated now in this time (the next year or less) that is Pleiadian. Whether you ever had any lifetime in past or future in that star system, the new human template—but it's you, it's not a hypothetical—the new human living calibration has this galactic strain of Pleiadian, along with 11 other DNA strands.

Pleiadians are not so comfortable in fourth or fifth dimension. They have other dimensional spaces. As their energy comes online for you, you at the hub—let's say you in the body here, and the energy body around that—have awareness now of Pleiadian activity, sometimes in the mental, sometimes in the emotional or energetic. You're aware of that flavor coming in. However, most of that is facing into a different dimension. You become like a walker of worlds; many worlds at one time. It's not a fractured feeling. But the Pleiadian part of you is not as comfortable in fourth or fifth dimension, so it will be leading you elsewhere in your perceptive abilities, and it will be speaking (so to speak) to you from a vantage point of another dimension.

This all comes in differently. From your vantage point, you may begin to perceive that it feels like guidance coming in, a sense of knowing. For some people, it feels like, "Oh, there's another being around I can see visually in my field" and for some it's that sense of noticing things in the built or natural environment that you had never noticed before, geometries in building structures, or different awareness of consciousness in plant life, trees, for example. These are some of the things that the Pleiadian DNA in you may begin to recognize. To be clear here, this is not a past life memory of you in the star system the Pleiades. It is the pure genetic strand of that type of star being in you, activated now in you.

All the tools we've been speaking about that are heart-centered and wish-centered still apply, because you are the hub of all of these activated parts of yourself. However, you become less one dimensional, even if that one dimension is fifth dimension. We go beyond hopping over to fourth, fifth dimension as a daily residence to, "oh yes, that's still the daily residence of the body self. However, I'm beginning to have abilities, perceptive insights and leanings towards other dimensions at the same time when I'm not traveling." You can imagine that this makes traveling easier, because when you do travel, you'll have those galactic activations within you, which will make it easier to perceive.

We'll give another DNA strand example here. Dragon is one of the galactic lineages here activated in you—one of the twelve. You can imagine that dragons have different value systems. There are many folklore tales about dragons and treasure for example. Well, what does that mean? It might mean that dragons are very connected with minerals of Earth and know how to sing them into being, for example. It also means on a physical, practical level, dragons have different types of eyes—the way cats and humans have different types of eyes—so they see color and light differently. Not only are they looking at different things that they value physically, they are able to see light and shade and mineralogy in different ways. So when you travel into dimensions—and dragons are also multidimensional—but when you travel into dimensions that dragons are at ease in, you will have now the physicality almost of the dragon eye to better see. It will influence your interdimensional travel; make it practically easier.

It's not that you can't travel now, but all of these things make travel in the future more and more concrete. Less of a special once in a while, and more and more "yeah, of course, I can go look into that dimension for the awareness that I need, where there are some friends to meet," something like this. So that you won't be so reliant, necessarily, on the guides who come to you, where they can influence the dimension that you are in by sending you messages or knowing or intuitions or clues or synchronicities. You can, in fact, go and visit some of these new and existing guides where they reside, and have a much fuller visual picture, a tangible sense of where they are coming from. Where does the wisdom they bring come from?

One of the more interesting parts of this, we feel, is that you begin to honor the human knowing, understanding how multidimensional it is. Because it is one thing to say, "well, of course, the Pleiadians must know more. I've seen books by them, and it seems they're very knowledgeable." And they are. They're very wise, by and large. However, humanity has that within them. And so you have not just one viewpoint. [You are] not limited to just what you might call human—old human on Earth, 10 years ago human. Now you have what in 20 years will be the normal human. And you're beginning already to flesh that out on a cellular level. It will include these dimensional awarenesses and perspectives.

You begin to see how vast the human potential is. Because it's not limited to just one of these. You can still admire what is the Lyran perspective, or the Pleiadian perspective, but not feel limited to that being higher or lower. You can have it all, essentially, as part of your human knowing. This is, by and large, one of the main reasons we have been working with some sternness with you around not putting knowledge outside of yourself, beginning to trust your own knowing. Because when you are leaned into the dragon part of yourself, or the Lyran part of yourself, or the Pleiadian part of yourself, in terms of that DNA strand, it's not going to be another being that's talking to you and saying, "Oh, I'm so wise and you should listen to my advice." It's going to be an instinctual or perceptual knowledge that you have, but may feel a little tingly, foreign, different, new, exciting, or all of the above.

We hope you won't be thrown into panic, but there may be some moments of discomfiture, of adjusting to this—these new eyes and this new vision, new way of perceiving. Because you are at the center now of 12 different new ways of awareness. And essentially these are being activated. You can activate them one by one, and some people are very knowingly, intentionally doing this—some guides on the planet right now, mostly human. And light language will naturally be activating this—light language from the solar codex, the solar light. Just being alive on Earth with the intent to ascend or expand into the new human potential, this is happening already.

It's all right if you haven't had dreams of yourself as a dragon, or haven't begun to think like a Pleiadian on some days. But then again, you might not know what a Pleiadian is thinking like, and that may be there already in your consciousness, streaming in and coming in with different types of art that you notice, and also different knowing. So the many, many dimensional aspects of this, as you expand in terms of the interdimensional wish field, it opens up quite a few different vantage points for what you might want to perceive, or heal, or see, or do in this life. And it also means that you have some pressure, in a neutral sense, towards the vantage point of that DNA strand, what they might wish for as a galactic whole.

For example, we spoke about dragons and mineralogy. You might find yourself wishing for mineral rich soil or certain types of treasure to show up in your life that really have not been on your radar screen before. That pressure comes from the dragon that's activating within you. From angelic standpoint, dragons are not mythical. They are quite real. There are planetary systems where they evolve and thrive. Dragons have not been so active on Earth as of late, but their DNA in the new human is there within you. A few moments down the road here, you might go and visit one of these planetary systems and visit some of the active embodied dragons who are solely dragon, and be able to telepathically speak with them. And short of that, or different than that, you might choose to just learn what that is through where your new tastes and leanings and perspectives lie.

Don't be surprised if you start to crave different things. Literally, this might be about food, but we're speaking more about art, knowledge, experience, types of music . . . You might find your perspective on what is interesting, good, natural, all of those may be shifting here in the next year or less, as the solar light activates these different centers within you.

To be quite literal here, to answer a question in someone's mind, no, you don't become like shape shifters. Some of you are that, but the new human in general is not a shape shifter, where you pop into a dragon shape, and then you look like a Pleiadian, and then you look like how you look to yourself now, more or less, with some years and wrinkles. But internally, these skills are active, and so they will begin to come online. You may have some moments of disorientation around vantage point, and that is all right; it's to be expected. Then you just come back to the heart of you in this physical, energetic self, and understand that you are the hub and the center of all this. And what you are is expanding—with light, in light—it is expanding, that's all.

You can choose to stay more limited to the you that you are familiar with and know. And also just know, at your own pace, you're going to have access to these other parts of yourself. Flashes of insight, visual pictures of yourself, let's say, as a dragon or Pleiadian might not be uncommon. That would be more in the third eye sight or the meditation or the dream space. You think "that's strange. I had a dream that I was a dragon." Because this DNA, although it's not a past life memory of you as a dragon, has that collective memory of that galactic type of being.

W*hat's the biggest advantage to having dragon energy? And related to that, is it okay to know the 12 strands of DNA that we carry? The dragons are surprising to me.*

This is Raphael. Yes, we will put out that list and also work with you little by little here as things come online. Those are the ones that are primarily coming online, softly right now. In the coming months, as things are more prominent, we'll speak more about those lineages. Angelic is one of the 12 strands of DNA. We are galactic in nature, and bound with humankind at this juncture in our history. In terms of benefit or neutrality of looking at these different components of yourself, the neutrality of looking at what is human is that all of these galactic types of beings collectively decided to share what is the best or the purest forms of their lineage—in terms of DNA—and what would happen if that was shared.

Certainly, you've seen this with plants or with usually just two races at a time of humans—how mixing can make something even more beautiful, enhance and take parts of each other. This is a bit more complex than the simple breeding, let's say, of two human mammals, because it's at the level of the DNA, so you have access to all of it. It's not that you have the earlobes from one and the nose of another. Yes, there are physical characteristics; but most of this goes deeper, more multidimensional than that. It's not to our mind that any of these are more or less valuable than the human that you started out with 10 years ago. But just notice that this is a different thing. You suddenly have access to these 12, in addition to your own history, your own lineage as human on Earth, of the older kind (not lesser, just older kind of human).

Much to be learned. But not to put perhaps one above the other. You might think, "oh, Angel must be better than dragon or Pleiadian." You get to have it all. That's what we mostly want you to know today, so that your wishes may begin to change. But also you can wish into these different parts of yourself and see how is a wish fulfilled in the dimension of dragons. So things you have been, perhaps, fixated on, for better or worse—ways you want to serve, or things you want to receive or have—become less important when you suddenly have so much access to so much different information and vantage points and skills and knowledge. Life as you know it begins to change quite dramatically. But from our standpoint, it's not that one is better or best—one of these 12 DNA.

C*an you get stuck in another dimension if you're not adept at interdimensional travel?*

This is Raphael. Your heart is here in the dimension where you reside. For now, for the next year or less, let's say that's fourth or fifth dimension. Wherever you wake up in the morning and you feel "this is home, this is comfortable," that's where your heart resides. If you're ever confused about where you are, particularly as who you are expands, you just come into the energetic heart space where you can touch the outside, where your heart is in the physical body. And just remind yourself, "I'm here. I'm right here." And you'll come back. Just don't force it, please. This modern society is so much about "what can I do in one minute or less?" Maybe it will take four or five minutes to come back. That's okay. So let it be gentle, but you can always come back to the heart and say, "okay, heart I want to be now in my physical self and bring me back gently there, please." As long as you don't rush it, you won't get stuck anywhere.

Is it still my soul?

Your soul has been many things. Some of you have had a lifetime as this soul in a dragon body or an angel body or Pleiadian body. And you happen to have been born as human this time around; but that's the same soul. The soul can be many things, and usually just one at a time, one life at a time. If you're believing in linear time—we'll keep it linear for a moment so this doesn't get too overwhelming.

When you become more aware, however, of the dragon-ness within you, within the new you, you could imagine that that might feel like it was some other part of you, like maybe a memory, or "I certainly wasn't born a baby dragon. So where is this coming from? It must be something walking in or exchanging right?" You can see where that understanding would arise.

From angelic perspective, it's still you. Nothing is swapping out. And it's still your soul. However, you have access to more energetic lines in this one life than would you ever have had before, or that any being has ever had before. Because this level of DNA genetic awareness, abilities is new.

Yes, there have been different types of hybrids in different galactic systems. But again, that's usually two, maybe three after the next generation of breeding. (Forgive the technical word, but it's the most succinct way of saying what we mean.) So maybe you have three races by the time a baby has another baby, but it's not the same, where you're right here in this one body, having access to all of it. And it's why the body has been going through such solar transformations, to hold all of this. It brings a lot of energy. It also takes a lot of energy. Some of you are finding that you need different fuel, food-fuel and so on, more liquids or different types of liquids to keep up with the energetic demands of everything that's coming in.

What are we supposed to do with all these DNA strands? How do we apply all this to our normal everyday life?

This is Raphael. Precisely how we do like to work is in the practical and the tangible. However, the more unlimited that you become, the less important, we would say, the practical will seem. But in the meantime, it's very important, because you don't want to feel that you have to go off into a cave and leave your life in order to become this so-called new human. This is happening as life goes on. And there may be disruptions, or maybe times when you're more tired, or times when you can't sleep because so much energy is coming in, so the more you can be a little fluid and flexible in your everyday life is best. But also it's gentle. It's not that you wake up today and you're one thing, and you wake up tomorrow and then you're all 12, and you have this disorienting overlap of impressions. It's coming online, so to speak, genetically online, incrementally, in sort of installments.

What you do with it is the same you would do with a new car, a new house, a new love. You try it out. You have fun. You see what it's like to live there. There's not an immediate call to action that you need to change your life or your food choices or your sleep. But some of this may naturally [happen]. Curiosities or insights may start to come up that feel a bit foreign to you. Always, you can ask your intuition, your guides. But also, we want you not to feel alarmed if different vantage points start to come in. You're not being taken over. Not to worry about different vantage points coming in.

That's quite a lot of mental energy here. We will absolutely be speaking in more concrete terms about all of this. For today, for now, we'd like to center with you a little bit, to give you an exercise, to help you to digest some of this. We'll offer this part also separately, so if you want to just have it on hand as a recording, if there are those times when you feel, "Oh, maybe I'm a little stuck in another dimension," or "I'm confused and overwhelmed" you have a tool to come back to centering and integrating all this.

2

THE NOW POINT

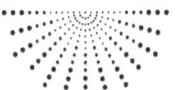

This chapter is the transcript of a meditation. English-language audio of this meditation is available free online with the link at the end of the book.

To engage with this meditation through the words below, invite the angels to participate with you using Angel Ariel's words as a focus. Pause in between lines or paragraphs to reflect or feel the energies.

This is Angel Ariel. Coming into awareness of the energy in the field all around yourself. This might feel like the air around your body, or the intangible energy that's in and through the body-self in the room you are in, or the outdoor space you are in.

It may feel like a bit of a hum or a buzz. It may have a sound to it.

Pulling all of that in towards the heart space. Noticing how all of the energy is anchored in and through the heart—the physical and the energetic heart.

The heart has a toroidal field which circulates. Taking all of that energy from around you, funneling it in and through the heart. Then the heart has its natural circulatory system in the energy field that is harmonizing and balancing what you have and what you are.

I am all of these energetic lines expressed interdimensionally in the Now Point. The Now Point is centered in the heart. I am fluid. And made up of all of these boundless energies, and sights, and insights funneled through the now. I am all of this, integrated fluid now.

The wisdom that I seek is within me at the right moment to flow through. The choices I see are perceived interdimensionally, in balance.

The energies I feel are taken from all of the dimensions I have access to and calibrated into now. In this heart. In this physical dimension. In me.

I am all that I seek right now. I have the energy for this, the insight for this now. And the exchange and interchange that I want to see in this now, the people and places and circumstance around me, multidimensionally.

I am right here at the center of this now.

Just breathing in the feeling of these energetic lines flowing in and through the heart. Breath is another way of anchoring the energies through and in now.

This energy and wisdom is alive in you right now, for your use. Not to catalog and file away, but for your use right now. Through the breath that is possible now.

Taking the energy you need from any of these dimensions into your now through the heart space, to balance and calibrate and flow with what you now are and what you now know.

The toroidal field of the heart distributing and balancing that naturally throughout your physical and energetic self that is now.

Right now in this space of you, in the heart, if a wish occurs (it's all right if it does not)—something you feel stuck with or you want to play with—resource your interdimensional self right now. Call in your resources to tangibly bring in this play or this unstuckness movement resourcing that you are seeking.

Breathing in and through the deep heart space of you. And letting that distribute through the toroidal field from the other dimensions of you into your energetic and physical now.

You've just pulled in the answer, or the playfield, or the resources that you called for through yourself.

Once again, coming to the awareness of the energetic and physical heart space and breathing in energies through those lines into and through the heart, into your now, through the toroidal field.

Energized with all that you are and centered into your now.

Keeping your focus on the heart, as you are ready at your own pace, fluttering open the eyes and becoming aware of the world around you that is gravitating, so to speak, right here around your heart. That is the center of all of this. Feeling the strength, the pull, of that.

Continuing to breathe as you integrate the inner and outer you.

You can spend a few moments at your own pace here integrating and feeling the balanced aliveness of you.

You can come back to this integration anytime you feel you're in rapid expansion, or you're a bit confused about who you are. Or you're a bit tired. Or a bit lost. You're drawing on your own resources, interdimensionally speaking, to fulfill your wish and also to come more present and balanced, calibrated to now.

3

CLEARING THE CLUTTER

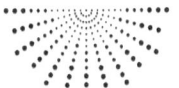

This is Raphael. Strong clearings are needed when new power is coming through dormant activated lines. You've had these beautiful channels dormant within you for many of your ancestral chains. We'll call it chains for the moment, not lineage. But you can think of it that way, if you like. In other words, through time there has been within humankind, the potential for galactic activation in these 12 types of galactic beings—the purity, or the intent to share their DNA, to cross-hybrid with one another to something called "human." The activation conditions have not been there for these potentialities to come fully online until just now.

So they begin. You are in the beginning of this. Two, three strands already alive, awake. And so like any plumbing or electrical wires that have been there—still in good condition, but not used for a long time —you dust things off, you blow some air through, let some sunshine in, whatever analogy works for you here. Clearing of the old crusty belief systems or old ways of leaning on. Let's say you were a three-legged dog, and you're used to having a crutch for a leg, and then suddenly you grow a new leg. Well, you clear the clutter of the old fake leg. Sometimes it's that you've been used to leaning on dormancy, or not using some of your skills. Clearing the clutter here, in this instance, can mean clearing out the sense of smallness. You don't need to think of it in terms of literal debris.

We're giving you a few different conceptual realities to look at here, so choose what works best for you. You don't have to hold them all in your mind.

Essentially, when new energies are coming in, you just want to make sure the conduit for that is well plugged in to yourself, connected, awake, alive. Then anything that then becomes extraneous, no longer needed, can be removed, let go of.

Some of this is what happened at the time of what you could call creation of humankind. Again, through the chain of lineage, some long time ago, your first ancestors, not necessarily through your bloodline, but we mean humanity starting out. There was some beautiful sense of hope. There was ingenuity. There was grumpiness and rage from at least one race involved. All of that can essentially be cleared as well, so that you have this neutral blueprint.

What do you want to bring to your 12 streams of activation? What's your blueprint? You might not like the energy of hope. Or you might not like the energy of rage. So we clear all of that. Because the intent, the emotional intent, or, let's say, the personas involved at that time are not relevant to you now. You don't have to be bound to what someone so many years ago was thinking or feeling or intending. You have chosen, as someone consciously ascending, to activate in yourself your full potential and then decide what to do with it. That's what we mean by neutral blueprint. You retain your free will to decide and kind of sweep away the personalities of those who were in the room, so to speak, at the creation of humankind.

We won't get into the technological aspects of the creation right now. But you can just think of it as an intent of 12 pure genetic strains coming into the hub of you. And you now are at the center of what to do next with all this information and activation—which will take a year or less. It doesn't all happen today at this hour, but we will be doing a clearing of all of the activated lines today. You don't have to know: "Well, do I have one activated or four activated? How do I know how to plug this in?" You can trust the angelic to do this for you, with you—with your hyper-conscious self.

You may want to redo this meditative process (clearing) periodically when you have this sense: "I think maybe another line just activated. And I feel a little like some clutter could be cleared. Some confusion is there. Or some old mess." So you might want to do this periodically over the course of the next year. It's not something you need to do monthly or daily, but perhaps four or five more times over the next year when you feel called. You can clear the clutter of the intent, the persona, the dormancy, anything that's leaning on limitation in your habitual systems of being. That's the intent today with the angels.

You may invoke us if you wish us to clear you. Just give your own assent (inside your heart or mind or out loud). Just so we know, should we work on you, with you today? Otherwise, feel free to just listen. We're asking you now in your own private space, to let us know, inwardly or outwardly: Are you on board with this clearing? Angelic clearing what is no longer needed to have a neutral blueprint, everything activated for the 12 strands of galactic within yourself. It doesn't mean they will all be active today. But to clear out what is helpful to smooth the way for you to then have free will to choose to do anything you like with this information, and with this energetic activation of you, your new skills.

And if you're not sure yet, you can read, and then you can read again, saying yes, if that felt good at a later date. There's no rush.

The rest of this chapter is the transcript of a meditation. English-language audio of this meditation is available free online with the link at the end of the book.

19

To engage with this meditation through the words below, pause in between lines or paragraphs to imagine, visualize or feel the energies described.

CLEARING MEDITATION

Coming now into awareness of the spinal column.

At this phase, although it is both larger and smaller, you might consider that these 12 strands of galactic DNA are running through and in the spinal column. They are part of the energetic central nervous system of you.

It's not important that you visualize them. We just want you to know they are there. So they're part of you. And like electric wires or plumbing tubing that does not always have something flowing through, they're just there—quite healthy, quite intact, with all of the information you need to activate all of your gifts and different perspectives of knowing and being.

Just breathing in the awareness that there's more there to you that you have yet to know, that is yet to become alive and awake.

Now allowing if you had said yes to angelic assistance here, the angelic golden light is flowing in from above the crown space of you, above the top of the head, the dome on the top of your head, above that. Angelic light is pouring through all the way down the spine and out the bottom of the spine into what you could call Earth.

Angelic light, at this moment, being called in as a clearing tool for any supports you have been leaning on that are keeping you from noticing or leaning into your new, empowered, embodied gifts—new ways of perceiving, sensing, feeling, acting, being. So that you have free-will choice to use all of the activated parts of you.

Breathing in that golden light and letting it filter down.

Angelic light is guided by your angels—personal and collective angels.

Angel Raphael and Gabriel are here to assist. Your personal angels may weave in and out of this as well to assist you personally.

Your mind doesn't need to know, your eyes don't need to see. We're just describing what is going on so that you can be aware while we are working with you. You may feel sensation at some part of the spine. It's all right.

You may perceive light or not; that's all right. None of this is required; but some of you are sensitive in different ways.

Breathing in and out deeply.

Just allow the light to flow. You're not in charge of the light. Just allowing the angels to do what they do best, to weave the light in and through, clear any passageways that are blocked, remove any stuck/stale information, matter, habits that are keeping you feeling limited and small. When in fact you have grown in ability and perception ability as well—sensory and physical ability and perceptive abilities.

Angels are holding you in light.

Some of you may have some visual flashes or senses of cognitive impressions. You don't have to give that too much importance. Because some of it might be trash moving out. You don't need to try to grasp at: "What is that?" Just let the impressions flow through and trust that the angelic is holding you in light. Any places of discomfort or mental dis-ease (anxiety), just breathe and hold your own love and light around that space.

Sometimes, when there's a deep spring cleaning, you've seen the animals in the house get all disturbed because they just want things to be quiet and how they usually are. But they're happy when the cleaning is done. There's an animal part of you that might feel like: "Wait a minute, what's going on? Why is there so much movement when I'm used to quiet?" It will quiet down again by the end.

Angels are holding you in light.

Light can burn and light can cool. So don't worry if you feel hot/cold sensations, or pressure, or flutters of light, or words, cognitive impressions. Any of that is expected depending on your ways of perceiving.

Now we're going to ask the angelic—the collective angels and your personal angels—to focus intently on those lines that are currently active, newly active in you from the 12 galactic strands of DNA, that they be unhindered by anything in you that wants to shut that down or say: "Wait, wait, wait. I don't do things the new way. I want to do them the old way." As long as you're consciously on board with ascension, angels are going to help to ease and smooth that transition for you. Particularly with how you interface, let's say (although you're not a computer, it's a good word here), with these strands of galactic DNA, so that it can be seamless and you can welcome those parts of yourself that are newly online.

If you want to have a focus here, if you're feeling frustrated trying to see angelic light and don't see anything, you could focus on the feeling or the word "welcome." Welcoming this new part of yourself, these newly activated DNA potentialities in you. Potentiality means it's awake, online, but you decide when and how to use it.

Welcome.

As any one strand (line) of DNA is complete, the angels will work on the next with you, the next active DNA strand. At this moment you might have three or less active and awake. Eventually there will be twelve. They do not all come online in the same hour; that's natural.

Breathing and "welcome" are your tools to join with the angels in this.

It is not important that the mind knows which. "Whose name is on this DNA strand? It is yours. It belongs with you, and in you. It is your activation. The mind doesn't need to know which galactic strand we're working on, because you have full agency and choice of when and how to use it. We just want you to have the ability to have it online.

Breathing and welcome, please. Light can feel like pressure; that's natural.

We're moving now to another strand within you (active, or soon to be active), weaving angelic light to bring this fully integrated with yourself with great ease and comfort.

Now sealing and clearing any of the remaining clutter/debris here, in the areas around these strands of DNA. Old blankets, even, things that were keeping you from seeing this was there so you didn't worry: "What is it?" Just wrapping that up and removing anything extra that's in the way of full activation here. There's no blocks in you. This is not what's being removed. It's more about the habit of leaning on the older DNA strands, and instead allowing your systems to look first at what's new and understand that more is available. Like opening the curtains and the sunlight comes in, more like that.

Breathing and welcome. And the angelic draining out anything excess through the bottom of the spine into Earth and ether. Burning up with angelic light anything extra, unused, clutter.

Completing our mission, angelic mission of clearing these newly activated lines with you, so you may give your thanks or acknowledgement. We're wrapping up in the energies and returning to your sovereign expression—your personal angels, your guidance team that is the most familiar for your day-to-day self. So the collective angels pulling back a bit. We are still "on call" should you want us or need us. But we are removing ourselves from being so actively intertwined in your field. Just breathe in, noticing you are sovereign in your space, in your energetic field. You are the hub. You control what's going on. You decide.

At any time, you can decide not to use what is active in you; the same way you don't always eat everything in your refrigerator, or walk through every unlocked door in your house. It's so nice that it's there for you, right? Convenient you don't have to walk through walls every time you want to move around in your house. Convenient that the food is there. But you decide the timing and how much, if at all, you access these gifts and ways of perceiving. That's up to you. Mind doesn't have to know what's there. We're speaking more to your heart-self right now. Just reminding you: You are in charge. You decide. Just because you have a gift, you may use it or not use it. There is ease now for you to do so more gently, more seamlessly,

Gathering yourself, your awareness of yourself towards the center of your heart space now. Angelic light has moved through your spine and finished, completed what it wanted to do today.

The heart space is your command hub for all of this. In the coming hours and days and months, when you're curious: "Hmm, what actually came online in me? What can I know about this? What new ways can I see and perceive reality, life?" You ask these questions, please, in the center of the heart, and not the center of the mind.

Heart is the command center for these 12 galactic strands. And the knowing is within you. You do not need to seek counsel or advice about how to do this, how to be a new human. You certainly may. It's helpful to compare notes. Why not? But you are not flawed and you are not imperfect as a human.

As you expand in your greatening human self, you have all of the tools to understand and know what to do next. That is part of the genetic upgrade that is inherent in the 12 galactic strand activations. You are in charge, and you do know what to do next. You don't have to know what to call it. You don't have to be familiar with it. But you can trust that these energies come with your ability to synthesize, integrate, utilize and welcome the new you.

Taking some deep breaths to just perhaps quietly within your heart space say to yourself to reinforce: "I'm in charge. I get to decide."

This is important because you're not coming into a networked system of someone else or something else telling you what to do. These galactic activations are not telling you who to be or how to be. They are simply expanding your universe.

Bionic man or bionic woman might be a good fun analogy here. Not that these are implants of any kind of technological nature; but in those stories that man and women were conscious beings who, just because they suddenly had extra strength in their arms or legs, they were the ones who decided how to use that extra strength. And it was already networked in their brain. They just tell their brain: "I want to crush this can" or "climb this mountain." And then the new arms and legs can do that, right? Or run so fast.

You're in charge. And you do know how and what to do next. Follow your curiosity in this. Playfully explore the new you. And it will, again, unfold in the next year or less. This is not an overnight transition.

You can expect new layers, new waves of being. And when you get new ones, you can come back to this meditation, to just ease and clear the way for that to come fully activated, easily. For you not to lean on the more limited way of: "This is how things are done" or "This is what I'm capable of." So like the newly minted bionic man or woman, you can with curiosity, ask: "Hmm, how much strength do I have now? Let me playfully try out and see." In this case, it's not so much about physical attributes as multidimensional ones: ways of seeing, perceiving, tasting, telepathy . . .

And we will be going through the 12 and some of their attributes, so you can learn to recognize the new parts of yourself. Today is just to open the expectation: You are in charge of all this. You are gradually becoming new, expanded. And you are still you. You will still recognize in you the core of what you might call the soul. You're still you. You are still the hub of all of these activations.

And that is, again, what we mean by you are in charge. You don't have to worry that suddenly some other galactic portion of yourself is going to start running your life. It's all you. It's just your capacity is great and different than what you knew.

4

CONNECTING THROUGH YOU

This Angel Raphael. We come right back into our theme of your expanding universe, also known as your expanding potentiality, your expanding self and knowledge of who and what that is.

We spoke about the 12 connection points you now have with your galactic self—some still dormant, some alive and awake, and some half/half waking up, like when you are in bed, yawning and stretching, not quite aware yet who or what you are. There's a mixture here. And it does take time. This is not sudden. You do not wake up one hour, one minute, and suddenly you are all of these new parts of yourself.

But you may find some shifts feel rapid, so occasional dizziness or disorientation about who and what you are is expected. Please don't worry about: "Oh no, did I lose myself?" If it continues on for many months, you can wonder about that. But for most of you, what's happening here is a transition and very natural to question at many stages along the way here: "Who and what am I?" and "What's going on right now?"

We'll speak a little bit today about this, and then activate a bit more with you as well. Before we speak more, let's begin to feel yourself in the field of you, and this is good to check in with yourself—doesn't have to be once an hour, but maybe once a day or less—to widen your perception of yourself as the hub that connects many different galactic potentialities, as we began to discuss last time.

If you think of yourself as a pillar, since the body shape of the human is essentially that way (when arms are down and you're standing up, you're essentially a pillar shape). Think of yourself as a pillar. You don't have to go into deep meditation or rest to do this—just notice yourself. And then widen your perspective a bit.

"What else am I? This is me as I'm used to thinking of myself—personality, cognition and so on—right here in this pillar." Essentially, this is within the spine, if you want to get technical, but it's fine if you think of it as your full body self around this pillar—which is the core of you, the cognition and awareness of you. There are 12 connecting lines collected into your belly button.

Don't worry so much: "Is this outside of myself, inside of myself?" Whatever comes naturally. Because essentially, it is both, because your energetic self is bigger than your body self, and this is happening on the subtle level. Some of you will see or feel this. Some we just want you to be aware what's going on, because these different personas, almost, or potentialities of you are you—they're connected in through the central pillar of yourself. If you become aware of yourself as this pillar, and there are 12 lines connecting in to the belly button, they are, you could say parallel, like a wheel around you. So if you are the hub or the center of a wheel, and there are 12 lines running through the belly button, down towards your feet and then up beside you, like much smaller columns all around you, essentially on the periphery of you are these 12 lines, energetic lines, that then connect in back through the top of the crown of yourself, of your central pillar. So they run from belly button up along parallel outside of your body-self, still in your energetic field, and then into the crown.

Similar, but not distinctly exact as the toroidal field around the heart. Similar, just not quite in the same place, or not quite exactly in the same shape, but quite similar. These lines form a field which is the wider you.

As all of these lines begin to come online, you'll feel a hum and an energy of the whole wheel, so to speak, although it's not rolling, but it is round—the whole wheel of you. It begins to hum and vibrate with light. You will feel that as the widening sense of who and what you are.

For right now, it might look like track lighting in a movie theater or airplane—a few strips of light around you. However you become aware [of this], as vibration or light. Some of these, maybe two or three of the 12, are active now.

And again, it's not so important that the mind knows: "How does that work? And what exactly is that?" As that you are aware you've signed up for some activations, some expansions of who and what you are. And we're giving you some context to understand and feel into what that is.

Any given time, maybe every Friday or once in a while, once a week more or less, you can check in which lines. How many lines are lit up? What's going on? Not so that the mind can keep track or check marks on a table, but so that you become used to acknowledging that you are changing and noticing when greater change arrives.

If you have one of these moments where you feel slightly unwell, dizzy spell, disorientation—you could stop and perceive: "Huh. Is another line lighting up?" Because if that correlates, then you can say: "Oh, phew. I don't have to wonder about what this sudden disorientation is. I'm just having another growth spurt. More of me is coming online."

Then the less you force, let's say, charging ahead with lots of activity or mental work at that hour, that would be lovely. If you can, give yourself the grace to relax into the widening hum of the energetic field around you. You are growing. With great certainty, you are growing in speed, power, sensation, nuance, magics of various kinds, interdimensional abilities, ways of being and so on. Those are just a few, to name a few of what you are now that's a bit distinctly new.

The mind wants to know, map it all out. What are they? Where do I go from here? And it's good to be in the practice of staying right in the center and in the present with this.

VISUALIZATION: I AM SECURE

When you want to feel: "I am secure." And we'll do this together now. You can bring your awareness to the belly button region and notice that there are these 12 connection lines. Some you may feel a hum, or see a light, and some, just like a thread or a spider web thread, you can almost see it's there, but not really, not anything happening there right now, or electric wire with no current running through. It's there, but nothing special sparking up around it right now.

That's quite natural at this phase. The security is knowing: "Ah, I'm all nestled in. I'm all locked in. I'm connected with, in other words, all of the parts of myself." And feeling that surety of the birthing into the greatening of you. Everything is in its right place, right order.

Birth moments, even if they stretch out over a year, are disorienting. Many of you remember some snatches of your birth, or you can imagine how disorienting it would be to move from water of the womb out to air—different temperature, different light, sounds are not so muffled, and scents are much sharper. A lot happens all at once in those few moments of birth, and it's disorienting. And that's all right. No one is expecting that you come out at that moment and feel: "Ah. Ho hum. Just had a birth. No problem."

It's not required of you that you enter this birthing of yourself, these different stages of activating, coming online with yourself—again, you're not a computer, but the analogies do serve well of some of that wording, like coming online—it's not expected that you enter this at each moment of the transition stages with bliss and calm and awareness of what's going on. None of that is expected at birth.

However, we want you to know that all is well. You're connected in all nice and snug with yourself. And those activations are occurring in two speeds or two activation points here. One is when you are ready. The first readiness was signing up to be born on this planet at this time. The second readiness was: "Yeah, I also want to change and evolve as humanity changes and evolves rapidly here. I'm not interested in staying in the three-dimensional version of humankind. Yeah. I'll go ahead and go through this very interesting time of change."

Then you're waiting, in a sense, for some of the solar and galactic light activations to hit Earth, to open up these portals, in a sense, to your own self, to your own energetic light. All of this is happening. You could say it was pre-planned, absolutely. At the same time, it's an organic process—how exactly and when exactly the sun flares. How exactly or when exactly you are ready to notice and extend those powers which are awake in you is also up to you.

There are many, many points of conscious intent, accepting and allowing at the same time as some are happening. Like the butterfly turning in to itself with wings instead of a caterpillar, some of this is happening without your conscious intent, just by who and what you are in this now. So both are true. Just because you have more powers active in you, with you now, doesn't mean you have to use them all at once.

Babies come when they're born with quite a lot of powers, you might say, that they don't really use all at once because they are disoriented. Then little by little, they start to be more active with some of those abilities they're born with.

31

There is no weakness in you if you don't right out of the gate walk into your powers and start using them and knowing what they are. Give yourself some moments to appreciate that this is a massive time of transition for you—for the planet as a whole, absolutely, but right now, we're focused on you.

Bring your awareness again to the belly button. There's a reason also why this shape is a bit like a ring or a wheel. And those lines of communication with your awakening self are right there and nourishment is also connected in through that region of your energetic self.

Good. So you're aware who and what you are, and you also really are not aware what all the nuances might mean. That is quite appropriate. Again, we'll come back to this analogy of the toolbox. If someone puts more tools in your toolbox, in your house—like a wrench and a spigot and a puddy knife and some screws and wall hangings—and some of them you've never seen before. You don't have to start using them right away. They're just there, and it's so lovely once you find out what they are. "Oh, I have more tools. I have it right here. Don't have to outsource. I know how to do this. I have the tools." It's a bit like that. You're widening your toolkit just by coming online with who and what you are.

Who and what you are in this context is not personal to your soul journey. We are not talking about remembering what your soul has done in the past or the future. We're talking about connecting with the pure galactic strands that weave together to form the new humankind. Humans will still essentially look the same—humanoid. You will likely not change how you appear to others and yourself so very much, except for those of you who have inner sight, inner knowing, you may start to see it in yourselves.

For example, we spoke last time about the dragon energies awakening. It will be quite obvious to some of you at some moments when your dragon is active, or someone else's dragon is active. Not that, like shape shifters, you suddenly look like you are a dragon, but you might see something in the light of the eye, or some quality that you come to associate with: "Ah, that's the dragon part." That becomes more natural to see that in others, and yourself.

However, those with third-dimensional, again, leanings or choices, you're not going to see anything different in you. You still look like you have two arms, two legs, hair on your head or not, and eyes and eyebrows and so on. You don't really change from looking in an external sense like a humanoid "old human." But there may be a glow to you, a knowledge to you that others who are going through this or have gone through this transition will recognize right away: "Ah, you decided to awaken. Great!"

This will help you, also, to calibrate your speech. Now we're speaking perhaps three to five months or three to five years from now. Part of the ambivalence you feel in communication right now with others is it's hard to know where they are in their journey. Is it polite to speak about these kind of things? Or will someone think you're nuts and want to lock you up in the funny farm? And when you can palpably see some of these qualities in others, it will be a bit like a secret handshake or a very obvious knowing: "Oh, okay, I can speak about these transformations, and you won't feel alarmed. You'll know what it is, it is in you as well."

Not secret in the sense of elites or hidden society. Again, this is open to every single human on this planet at this time. However, some are choosing not to embark on such a big adventure in this life. They'd rather hold off. From the angelic perspective, it's beautiful to respect that, and also not judge it. There are reasons to stay in the third-dimensional planes in this life. Why not? You can choose anything you like. But we speak to you now as if you have chosen to move into this ascended self, this ascended version of yourself.

5

WHAT IF I DON'T FEEL IT?

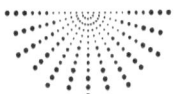

Can I ask a question about the transmission? You had said, check in once a week, or check in anytime you feel dizzy or kind of out of it to see if one or two of your lines are activated. Okay, but if you don't know what they are then how is that helpful?

This is Raphael. It's more learning to focus on what you see. The first time you looked through a telescope or binoculars and someone's saying: "Don't you see it? It's right there—the nebula, whatever, this planet." And you think: "What am I even looking for?"

And yet, if when you look again and again, finally it comes into focus and you see. Or you get the trick of how far or near to be from the telescope or binocular. It's more like that. Then we say tune in and see. "Well, what do I notice now?"

The first several times, you may not notice anything, but you are developing a little bit of a baseline with yourself. If you notice: "Oh, wait, there's something over here that feels different or looks different than it did last month. Maybe this is a new line coming on. Having

35

that interest, you don't have to be adept yet at understanding what you see or seeing anything yet.

Just having the interest to look in that direction, some of you are visual, some would have more of a feeling, sense of what's different. "Is this just me in the old paradigm, or are parts of me coming online?" Within the context of how we described the energy lines moving, you may not see that or feel that. Just tune into that. "That's what I want to be aware of within that energy system. Are things changed? Is anything new today?" Some of you may know something at that moment, or hear something, or see something, or smell something, and then not know what that means. "Hmm, different smell. I don't know what that is."

Not being impatient to know right away what it is, or how to interpret the imagery. Like scientists who could see through the telescopes, the first ones, they didn't know what they were seeing yet, right? It took some while to understand what was gaseous energy in space, what was a planetary binary system and so on. It won't take you as long as all of that, but don't expect to know right away, to be able to interpret what you see, or know in a felt sense: "Oh, I do feel something."

The angel said that we were already everything that we're going to be. It's just that we're kind of going through it like the metamorphosis to become that. So if we're already what we're going to be, then what good is wishing if it's already done?

This is Rafael. We're speaking in that particular context about dormancy coming to life. When you speak about DNA or other kinds of activations, it's something that's in you. Just like the tree is inside the seed, the big, marvelous tree inside the tiny seed, all of that potential—the skills, the nuance of your gifts—is there within you.

However, even once that's fully manifest, what are you going to do with all of that? That's where your wishes come in. You might decide.

"I don't want to use any of these gifts. I want to go back to structural, slow thinking life." We don't think you'll choose that, but you could. Or: "Well, I want to go have a galactic focus, interplanetary exchange." Or: "I want to focus on Earth and her pollution." Or: "I just want to play in my yard and see the beings that are there—use my skills for that. The way I say 'hi' to my neighbors, I'll just say 'hi' to my galactic and fairy and dragon neighbors in my yard instead."

There's still so much choice, and that's where the wishes come in. But what's inevitable here is if you have chosen to ascend that will unfurl, just like the tree coming out of the seed is inevitable when conditions are right. And conditions are right for humankind to unfurl.

6

UNIFICATION & PEACE

This is Angel Ariel. We speak now to that in your nature which feels it wants to change, but does not know how to change. You are what you are already. Like the pillow inside the pillowcase, all the stuffing is there already. You don't have to inflate up or down or become something other than what you are. All of this is inside of yourself. Right now you have the change agents and the new abilities and perceptive tools that you wish to use when you want them.

This is not about impatience, but about the fear: "Do I have what's in me? Have I done enough to foster the recognition of who and what I am? Have I done enough to awaken?" This is not a doer situation. It's not about effort. You can relax into what is literally in your DNA structure—has been there, is now awakening.

You don't have to do anything, earn anything, elevate in any manner to own this and be this. You are this multidimensional version we are calling "new humankind" because it's quite distinct, as you will come to see in the next year or less—quite different from what you once knew in terms of: What can a human do? What can a human perceive?

Particularly those two things. Not so much that the intent of you will change—why you came to this life or how you are with other people. But your ability to shape the world and know that that is the case. And your ability to perceive in multi directions, which is an essential ingredient to peace.

When you are looking at the world through only one vantage point, it is difficult to find peace with another, let alone galactic societies or other nations or other races on Earth. When you have so many varieties of perspectives within you, it does not feel like a push pull of: "Which one of these do I choose?"

It feels like looking through a prism or a jewel with many facets. There is a glory to being able to see all different ways all at once. And we call that unity, and we call that peace. The peace that you seek for the world, your world at this hour, is within you. And the more that you rely on your awakened self to know and perceive in multiple ways, the quicker humankind reaches the unity, the unification of peace—which is not the unification of sameness. Not: we all wear the same color, hair, skin or uniform, think the same ways, have the same thoughts. But that we see—like many facets of the same jewel—we are all of conscious intent.

Harmony arises, arrives when you stop trying to make everyone else look through the portal of one fixed viewpoint, and allow that there are many facets of the gem of humankind. And the rainbows, the nature, the life at different phases, the different foci of humankind are allowed to exist all at once in what you might call peace—unification.

You are blessed beyond measure. From angelic perspective, you are blessed beyond measure to be part of this unification, this peace, which includes multitudes of perspective, understanding, dance, color, light . . .and is not about forcing into one unique viewpoint and the sameness of all.

Part of what you're seeing in global politics right now is the stark contrast of what is the opposite of what humankind is moving into.

We're not saying that every politician has this view right now, but you see some of this—the old way of enforcement: It must be one way, one viewpoint, one homogenous self. And that is what felt, at some point in time, safe for humankind.

Now you move into what feels again, anchored in through the belly of you, belly button insert point there, all of these 12 perspectives with you as the hub. "Ah. What is safe is I am all of that. I'm anchored in that." So it is a wisdom. It is a waking up to who you are. And not a fine tuning, a sharpening of who you are, but a widening. Like a beautiful lotus opening up. Humankind has much to awaken to, and much that we admire being able to bear witness to in you. You are blessed to be a part of, to be the most active part of what is going on for humankind on planet Earth right now.

This is not about galactic beings in spaceships (or coming through the belly of mountains) to come "save" humankind. This is not about angels coming with so much information and light to "save" humankind. This is about humanity waking up to something she never knew she was, which is the most glorious creature we have yet to witness. You are blessed to be that.

We stand alongside you. Angelic is one of the lines of galactic DNA, intertwined as part of your humankind. You may also begin to stand in light with what you are, with the resonance, with the purity of the angelic. Not the part of the angelic which is the polarity of light. You all know of some of that history. But the purity of the angelic. The angelic without the dual point.

Collaboration and community are two of the gifts that the angelic brings to your new human self. It's not that you didn't have those qualities in the older version of humankind, but you stand in the light of those in a way that is quite brilliant and brave now. And you will see that that goes a long way to forging new societies and new light on Earth with a lot of ease and comfort. Well, that is part of what you have access to from the purity of the angelic genetic strand— collaboration, community.

41

Coercion is out with the old, right? Nowhere in this blueprint we have described is there a hierarchy of humankind. Each being, as we have said, has access to this. You didn't have to be judged as worthy. You are that.

7

DO I NEED TO LET GO OF WHAT I WAS?

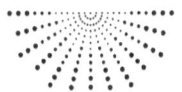

This is Angel Ariel. When you take on so much that is new in terms of who you are to become—based on your own wish field, but also a whole nuance and very blatantly, obviously different set of skills and perceptions, ways of viewing the world (quite literal, ways of viewing the world)—what place is there for the persona and the soul learning and those parts of yourself that you hold dear from this soul's journey in this life (this life path and others, concurrent life paths)? What place is there for that expression of yourself as you have known yourself so far?

You had some skills in your 20s, 30s, now. You've become accustomed to: "Am I psychic or not psychic? Can I communicate telepathically? Am I tall or small? Do I view myself as a leader or a follower or both? Sometimes both. Am I collaborative in nature? Do I hoard things or am I more generous? Do I gift away, or both?"

Many different ways of viewing a soul and a pattern from this life and other lives (concurrent lives) that you've come to hold dear. Because those are, let's call them, your value systems. That's how you live. But also they are what you might call your parameters.

43

Based on the sort of vehicle that you have in this life—your body and your energetic vehicle—you come to understand what the parameters are. In other words: limitations and growth potential and the things you do best. Now, all of that is about to change. And you have undergone some of this change already.

What, if anything, of what you know of yourself, do you need to leave behind? Is it important to have an ego death? Some people call it that. Is it important to redefine the structure of who you are? And how much do you need to change into what you now have license to use?

ENERGY CHECK-IN

Take a moment to just notice yourself, where you are. This is different than what we did last time. Just noticing your body, where you are—just lightly, loosely aware of what you might call yourself. Some of you are very aware of the energetic self. If you're not, you can focus more on the body self, or some combination. Just noticing that you are. Right now in space and time, you are.

This combination of what you can perceive is you. Does it need to change? Does some of it need to go away or be left behind?

The short answer is yes. And the long answer is: it depends. The timing depends on you.

Since we use the word vehicle for your energetic self, and you're aware now that you have 12 new strands of energetic self, essentially, coming into activation. If you had, in the past, had only one vehicle, it's very clear that's what you're going to use when you drive to the shops. If you're gifted or inherit or buy three or four more vehicles, and you have those in your garage, it's not as clear when you go out which one you're going to ride. And over time, let's say the newer ones, you become accustomed to their features. You like how the sports car drives. Or you like how the big family van can carry a heavy load. You have access to those different vehicles for different types of adventures or practicalities.

Eventually, the car that you used when it was your only car, you do phase out. You stop using it. The features are not as nice and new or capable as the new ones. Whether or not you keep it around, it's not that important. It's not in this case that you have to give up yourself in order to receive a new self or expanded self. But as you recognize all of these new ways of being that you're coming into, you're going to find that your original self from this life—let's call it the energy vehicle—it's outmoded.

When you get the new phone, for a little while you're attached to the old one, because you knew how it worked and the color scheme and the wallpaper you'd chosen and all that. And the cover doesn't fit the new phone. And then after a while, sometimes only an hour or a day, oh, boy, you can't imagine how you ever functioned without the new skillset that's in your phone.

It's not a matter of being forced, or a grievance to the old self. But you will want to, we would suggest, leave it behind. At some point it just becomes superfluous when "I'm really not using this anymore, the old way of more limited thinking, the old way of not having telepathy, perhaps limited or no psychic ability. . ."

Yes, you will leave behind what you have come to know of yourself. But the you that is your soul is still driving. Then similar, in the analogy, it's still you driving the different vehicles, right? The family car, the sports car, or the car you used to drive, it's still you driving; but you have different vehicles.

The energy lines coming into you now, you could think of them as different energy bodies. Although, it's not that you're walking around with 12 bodies. That's where the analogy falls a bit short. But it is that dramatic where you may feel: "Well, I'm still driving, but this is a different thing that I'm driving. Because it knows how to do so much more. It perceives differently. I have these new skills, although I'm not quite sure yet how to use them."

The older way of you does fall away. And you can—when you're ready —do clearings to essentially disengage from that energetic self. Or you can keep it around for the rest of this life. There's no urgency to leave it behind.

We don't ascribe to the fact that you need to die to your sense of self as an individual—your tastes in music, or art, or what you like to eat .. . Although that will change. The body changes. But you don't have to forcibly give that up. It may naturally happen that way. Yourself as a soul signature stays the same.

Again, to the analogy of how you are when you drive a sports car versus how you are when you're driving the family van, maybe a slightly different persona in you comes up. The more playful driving a sports car, the more practical, need a different type of parking space if I'm in the family van. But it's still you, right?

You will have perhaps more aspects of yourself to explore and enliven. But you're not going to find that you become something else—a different sort of automaton, or some other consciousness that's more wise or just different than you that takes over. It's not like that. You are not being asked to give over, to surrender and have something else take over.

Yes, that does happen—willingly or unwillingly—being taken over can happen. But that's not what we're suggesting for the New Earth self. It's still you in charge. Your agency around making wishes and so on; it's still highly important that you're the one doing those things. It's just you're going to have access to a lot more *oomph* behind actualizing, manifesting, watching things happen in your world, shaping society at large, and viewing these things with more pinpoint precision. What's going on in the world <u>really</u>? You can see it more readily/easily. These are the kind of things you can look forward to.

It's still you, and you don't have to worry about some unfamiliar oversoul or wiseness of yourself or ancient lineage coming in to live out the rest of your life. No, you're here. You've earned your right to continue to be here in your life and to enjoy this time of immense change. For most of you, that's why you chose to be born in this era. Not the only reason. You had babies to be born from you, and people to meet, and passions to follow in your work and life. Of course, being here right now, after so many decades alive, is not your only reason for being here. And yet, if you are still here, this is a big reason, one of the reasons you came in to this life.

It's your right to enjoy it. It's not some other consciousness, even some aspect of you that's going to come in now and take over and get to enjoy the unfurling of this beautiful, adept, new self of you.

8

ARE THE 12 THE SAME FOR EVERYONE?

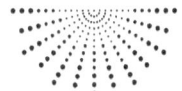

The 12 strands, as I understand it, there are some, at least, that everybody will be having—the angelic, the Pleiadian, the dragon. Are all the 12 the same? Or does it vary between individuals?

This is Angel Ariel. The template for the New Earth Human is the same for all. However, you still have your soul leanings and soul concurrent lifetimes. If you had in what you might call the past been a Pleiadian, you may be much more interested in accessing that line more often, because you have also soul memories in addition to the purity of the galactic strain of DNA itself. Whether or not you've had a lifetime as a dragon, Pleiadian, angel, you each have access to those three strands, and the other of the 12 will be the same. But you are not all the same as souls. Some of you will have had lifetimes that are not in these 12 so you have access to additional memories. And sometimes—this is soul specific—sometimes you do bring skills in with you to another lifetime. Or at some point you open up to remembering: "Oh, I know how to do this. I've done this before."

The 12 is not limiting, but it is specific. The way you could say the human DNA structure now, it's clear that for most people, anyway,

49

you grow 10 fingers, 10 toes—there's certain similarities with the human self as much as there are differences. The 12 strands will be the similarity. However, you decide how much to access some of the 12. So some of you will be in the dragon energy a lot, and some might touch it once or twice and say: "That's okay. I know it's there, but that feels too big or too protective for me or something."

There will be a lot of choice in this. However, the template for the new human is the same for each human. Soul is not the same. The template you could think of as the energetic self. That's why we've been calling it a vehicle today. The soul is in the energetic self driving; but the energetic self will have the same blueprint for all of the new humans.

With all of us getting all the same strands, what is the time frame for that? And is it the same time frame for everybody? And are we talking angel time (i.e. decades)? Are we talking human time (i.e. couple of years)?

This is Adria. Angel time is sometimes very specific, but often is more of a guideline. Sometimes when they say one month it means one to four months, as opposed to three years from now. I use it as a sort of a guideline: near term, medium term, long term.

Yes. This is Raphael. Angels are not in time. As an aside here, when you're accessing the angelic strand of your DNA, you have the capability to move without so much time pressure. Many of you will enjoy that.

In terms of when, it is available to all now. Very few are beginning the process now. Within this year or less—seven to 10 months more or less—a wide portion of humankind will begin this activation. There's nothing you need to do to press the start button. But as we had said, the acceleration of the energies on the planet do make the conditions right for things to start to come online. And then once you've begun the activation process, again, 12 months more or less, to complete the process, so that it's not so mind-bending, really.

There's a physicality to it, but you have been doing much of the physical adaptation already to prepare for this. But it is quite a lot for the mind and those parts of perception of you to integrate all of these new energetic lines. That's why the integration will take some time. That's out of compassion, not that you need to be struggling through. Like unwrapping so many centuries of presents all at once—hard to do in one hour, one day. So about a year for that.

R*ight. And that would be all the people on the Earth? So those still choosing 3D will also have this available, whether they take advantage of it or not?*

[Angel Raphael:] Yes. Exactly yes. It is not a chosen few or something you have to earn. However, there is a free will opt in. For those who, at this moment, are choosing to live out the rest of their life expression in this life story in third dimension with polarities and so on, and lower density overall, their choice will be honored. And if they change their mind some moment, they have some sort of awakening or change of heart, then they can go right into this process.

Let's say, four years from now, someone says: "Oh, wait a minute. I've seen so many of my relatives and friends. . . I don't know what's happening to them, but I want that." Then they can begin the process themselves, just through opting in.

The energy has to rise to a certain frequency on Earth for the conditions to be right for this. But then there's that extra step of opting in, and that's where either before you came into this life, many of you essentially already opted in at that time. "Okay, when this happens, sign me up for that." And then, of course, you can still change your mind to opt out, or you could still change your mind to opt in, even though you weren't sure coming into this life. That will remain open. A few people are beginning that adventure now. But for most of the people who have opted in, it will be seven to 10 months from now to begin. [recorded April 11, 2025]

What is the best way to activate the new strands?

This is Raphael. It does happen on its own, although there are people who knowingly or unknowingly perform activations, and that word is trending now. It is possible to activate them early. However, we're not inclined to advise that you do that just now to try to activate all 12 all at once. We have been working with you to begin to activate and bring those online sooner than later. However, it is absolutely not necessary that something external, other than the conditions on planet Earth that create the frequency match for this. It's not important or needed to activate these lines, but what we're doing here is smoothing the transition, smoothing the pathways and giving the contextual information. Because when you're ready, or when this is ready on the planet, it's very helpful to know what's going on. Or you might start to wonder why your value system and perception is changing so rapidly and day to day is moving all around, and why suddenly you have telepathy and other fun gifts of perception and sight.

Will we know consciously which of the cars to take out of the garage on a particular day? And by that I mean: say our intentions, our particular things, or our wishes—will we need to know which of the strands we're tuning into to make that happen, or will it be automatic?

Quite automatic. This is Raphael. There's two ways to go about this, two primary ways. One is when you have the intent: "Oh, today I want to move energy." Or: "Today I want to telepathically connect with someone around the world," or something like that. That part of your skill set can come in and open up, be used, without you necessarily knowing: "Was that Pleiadian in me? Was that dragon?" and of course, some of the galactic strands will have similar, overlapping . . . let's say multiple of them will have telepathic gifts, but they might be slightly different in the way that they're perceived by you.

The other thing we would suggest, as you playfully encounter this, is sometimes like when you want to take out the sports car and just see what it can do. You don't really have any particular place to go or vision in mind, intent. You can intend to spend a day with your dragon self. What is that? What is it like? And then, in that way it will be both, we would say. But you don't have to worry about . . . it's not like you have to read a big instruction manual in advance. " right. In order to activate telepathy, I have to go over here to this channel and press this button, or say these words, and then telepathy will be on." It'd be more fluid than that. So your intent. And then, of course, just trying things on. Some things will be like trying on a new dress, does it suit you or not? And some things would be like trying on new gardening gloves or something, you know how is it different, using your hands with those tools. With the gloves on it feels a bit different, but you can do some things easier. It'll be a bit of both with the gifts as well. Some things you just might not care for very much. And some things take just a little getting used to. But you don't have to mentally know so much about them.

Like garden gloves—most people don't read a manual about how to use them, but it's a bit odd sometimes first time you wear them.

9

THIRD EYE ACTIVATION

This chapter is the transcript of a meditation. English-language audio of this meditation is available free online with the link at the end of the book.

To engage with this meditation through the words below, invite the angels to participate with you using Angel Raphael's words as a focus. Pause in between lines or paragraphs to reflect or feel the energies.

This is Rafael. We ask you each to come into a focal point of what you might call the third eye. If you need a reference point in your body self, it would be around the center of the forehead, in between the physical eyes. Somewhere like this, more or less. You can, some of you, feel sensation there, when you think of it. Or you might have seen pictures of someone with three eyes. It looks like that. The third eye is not a physical eye, but it is a way of perception. We are going to activate that center with you today, because many of the galactic strains make use of quite nuanced inner sight. And if this center in you is active and awake/alert, it's easier for you to then integrate the visions that you see, and to see with that much nuance. We'll bring our focus there. Please don't worry about

55

exactly where on your forehead. You just have the sense of bringing your awareness there.

Recognizing in yourself that you have much more to see in this life. That there have been things behind the scenes—in other dimensions, in the one you're in, and future and past. That you have perhaps not accessed your ability to see, or did not feel you had the ability to see just yet. Recognizing that in yourself there is a visual center where you can see frequencies of light and shadow--so shapes and color-- and give it meaning. The way your physical eyes connect with the brain--they give meaning to what they see. We're also activating those channels that give meaning between the inner eye and your centers of ways of perceiving in the brain space and other ways of knowing. Not quite so clear as a conduit from the third eye to the brain, but that's the idea. Also all of your parts of knowing connected with all of your ways of seeing.

Asking the angelic please, if you wish, to come in and clear and purify any misperception tendencies in your inner eye area. The way you might correct a cataract or other eye failing in your physical eyes, you can ask the angels to come in and just clear up anything that might be skewed or misperceiving in any manner, so the eye can be clear and neutral and give you precise information. What you do with the information is up to you.

Asking the angelic to come in and clear that conduit and channel for sight.

Allowing that light or pulsation may be there. Or just a knowing that the angels are at work, at play, in clearing, and transferring any misperceptions out of that field of perception, of sight. So that you can have precise detail that translates to knowing without interference or distortion.

So that you may see what is. What you do with that is up to you.

Remembering to breathe. This energetic inner eyesight is very networked in with the physical self, so it appears to be essentially inside your forehead, more or less, and a bit on the outside. Just breathing as this is cleared for you.

For some of you, this eye is quite large, so don't be alarmed, or don't try to censor/edit if you feel like: "I don't know, I feel sensation over most of my forehead." You don't have to pinpoint it. For some of you, this perceptive ability, even if dormant, is quite large.

It is not the same size as the physical eyes, and it does have an aperture, so it can expand and contract according to the scenario on whether you are looking with your inner sight or not. You can close this eye, the way you can close a physical eye. It doesn't mean shutting off the conduit, but attempting not to see for a moment. Or having a rest. You have that ability with this sight as well.

You might practice that right now, if you like. It does not need to look like an eyelid. It could be more like a screen door, a sliding door. Tune in a little bit to the fact that there is an off or a rest mode for this way of seeing. That's important. Just notice that you have that as well.

Even if you can't see anything with that eye right now, you could feel how restful it feels to draw the eye closed. And how there's more energy there when you intuitively think: "All right, I think it's time for that to be open." You can feel there's more energy—maybe a sense of light, or color, shape. You don't have to try to interpret what you see right now. Just notice the difference a few times back and forth. What it's like for the eye to be open, and then that beautiful rest and soothing sense of quiet when you can also gently close the eye.

A few times, opening and closing, so that you know that once you begin to have sight you're not stuck with seeing visions all of the time.

Perhaps one more time open and closed.

Asking the angels to add a layer of light that helps you to interpret what you see as you're getting used to this coming online.

And enjoy. If there's any sensation or light there, just enjoy it without having to interpret right now: "What is it that I see?"

"Oh, something feels or looks just a little different. How glorious!"

This is Raphael. We will continue in the following chapters with this mix of context and practical tools to ready you as you ease into these transitions. Please do practice and contemplate.

1 0

WAYS OF SEEING

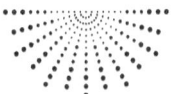

question please. They mentioned if you have a cataract, that will also be physically healing the eye, if I understood it correctly. Should I listen quite a few times to the third eye activation, or has the healing been ignited?

This is Adria. I heard that as an analogy, not as literal about the cataract in the eye, but that the third eye, if it has a bit of a covering, you're just removing it. Let's ask them about that.

Yes, in this case, both. This is Angel Raphael. When you open the third eye or enact visual representations that come into being it does affect vision in the world. For example, conceptually you know about vision boards, or envisioning something in your future and then it comes into being. Let's say, in an Old Earth way it could have been through planning. Or you could just receive it now in New Earth (again, more quickly, more readily than you imagined back then). But through envisioning then it comes to being in your world.

Even if it's through hammer and nail and many years of effort, the house then comes into being. And then you can see it with your eyes.

59

In a practical sense, what you envision you then later see in your reality.

When you remove blocks in your envisioning—and here we mean more specifically, the third eye, or more abstractly, your way of visualizing other information (if it's from other dimensions or from your guidance team)—that does have an effect on the physical eyesight as well.

When people talk about seeing clearly, you know that's often about a mental standpoint, and not just 20/20 vision. Similarly, if you have something going on with your health, including your eyes, if you have an opening in your ability to envision through your third eye that will affect your ability to see the solution.

That's a bit different than saying if you clear your third eye, your vision will clear—if you're short sighted, suddenly you're not short-sighted anymore. However, if you clear your third eye and your focus is on your short-sightedness, you may have a vision—a flash of knowing how to handle your short-sightedness, whether it is through healing, vitamins, surgery, eyeglasses, or eye muscle exercises, something like that; many different approaches, depending on the individual case. And certainly you can call in healing. But in your case, we would say when you're looking at cataract and its relationship to third eye, you can envision your cataracts becoming clear, and either they will because they're responding to your wish, which is the most likely scenario in your case, and or you will receive insight about what eye drops, what practitioner, what medicines might work best for you. And it may be a combination. So, yes, you can directly influence your sight through third eye, but more commonly, or more broadly, as New Earth often is the case—instead of, for example, wishing for money so that you could buy the house, if you just wish for the house, it could come in many ways—if you wish through the third eye for eye healing it may come directly through third eye vibrations. It may also come through insights that the opening in the third eye brings to you. So direct healing or insight/information. Insight has the word sight in it, right?

Can I ask if it's good to listen to that transmission a few times, or was it enough to do it once?

Absolutely. This is Raphael. Follow your inclination in this. We would say for you, yes, there's a few more layers there, if you like, and not to be afraid of what power and empowerment that might bring. Because for most, third eye is about perceptive ability. For you, there is a transmission out as well. It's like a two-way eye. Some people have that where they're able to gift energies outward. That's where we see your trepidation or instinct towards power being known soon in yourself, nothing to be frightened of but you can take your time exploring it.

People who have that gift, is it that they can heal others with the outward expression?

Light, in this sense, is neutral, a neutral force. This is Raphael. If you picture a lighthouse—like a beam of light outward—that's what we would say is a visual concept you could lean into. And then be neutral at first about what that light might bring to others. It is about others.

There are many uses, potential uses. You can paint with many colors. It's not only one thing. Like voice or song, it has so many different ways it can be used. The light from the third eye also has many adaptations, many uses.

I do wonder when the 12 galactic strands are all active, and we have access to all these new parts of ourself, will we come into a firmer sense of new identity that isn't changing often?

Yes, absolutely. This is Raphael. Let's say you get new suitcases. You arrive at a resort destination, or whatever is fun for you—for some of you that's out camping in the woods, but for now, let's just say a resort destination—you arrive and someone has told you: "Oh, your wardrobe is all packed. Food is taken care of." You have all of these suitcases with lovely belongings that you haven't opened yet. As you go through, sift through those, and wear those and different seasons come about, you start to settle into what is still new, what is still lovely, but you can settle into that identity. It's not that every week or every month those bags are taken away, and now you have a whole new wardrobe (in this case, the analogy of all of your skill sets and ways of perceiving). It's not that you wear them all all at once, or get tired of them quickly, but there is a brand new you all the way through. A new you. It will take some time to get accustomed to, but it doesn't continue to change.

Now you as a soul can continue to evolve. Or you might rest a while or enjoy/play. That's up to you. As it was in Old Earth, the soul still has its journey, and you get to choose that moment by moment. But in terms of the metamorphosis of the energetic and physical, physiological, perceptive selves, that will reach a culmination. We won't say a plateau, because you can continue to grow as a soul. But the transformation will reach a culmination.

To go back to the analogy of a butterfly, your wings will be formed. You'll know how to fly. But where do you fly? What are the different blossoms and how long or short of a life do you have left? What do you do with it? That part's up to you. That's the soul's journey.

And so life is still precious, fleeting, changeable. And yet you are new. You will have all of this, your wings fully formed, so to speak. The butterfly doesn't continue to transpose itself into yet another kind of being and another kind of being . . .Once the metamorphosis is complete, it is that. It doesn't go back to being caterpillar. It doesn't molt and change its wings. There is a transformation which is one-way, and which will have a culmination. Then you are not complete in the sense that the life journey is not over and done, and the soul journey is most likely not done. You're not just going to be in stasis as a soul. You still explore, experiment, gift, receive . . . all of that.

O*ne of the things they mentioned was about the third eye having some connection with being open to some of the galactic downloads. Did I interpret that correctly?*

Absolutely. This is Raphael. In a practical sense, telepathy—when you're speaking about physical galactic beings, not your galactic DNA —telepathy will be the primary source of communication. And telepathy is visual and knowledge-based. It's sort of like a movie where you know what the meaning of the movie is. Not like a dream, where you have to interpret what these images might have meant. Having a third eye quite open does help with telepathic understanding and communication, both. That's about communication, direct communication with other life forms present now in this life with you, absolutely. Third eye opening does facilitate that kind of communication.

It also helps you to see interdimensionally. Some beings will come visit you in the dimension you are in. Some beings you go visit them in their dimension, or you peer into their dimension. Third eye is very helpful with that also, to be able to perceive. Some of you have traveled interdimensionally already, but don't necessarily see what's going on. You might feel it or hear it or know it. It does enhance your ability to know what's going on, to be able to see interdimensionally, as well.

I*s there no limit to how much, how open, and how amazing your third eye can be? Is that an infinite possibility?*

In a sense, yes. This is Raphael. When you think of ultimately, how many combinations. Now if you think of the physical eye, 20/20 is sort of a benchmark of that's very good or perfect vision. But some people see beyond that—both in short and far vision, can have clearer or better vision than that.

Similarly, there is sort of a baseline of what is good, clear third eye vision. And some people will see even beyond that, in both far and near. Also, there are ways of perceiving through the eyes. We had spoken about the dragon galactic strain and that way of viewing the world. When you are looking through the third eye through one of the lenses of the galactic strains, that's one combination. If you're looking through the third eye through Lyran or Pleiadian perspective, that's another—different ways of combining information. That's how it becomes unlimited. It's not that there isn't a limit to what the third eye can see, but because of the combination of the galactic lens plus the clarity, you can do unlimited ways of perceiving through the third eye. And then so many landscapes to be met interdimensionally and in the dimension where you live.

It would be like seeing one or three countries and saying: "Well, I've seen all there is to see." Not really. There are other places to see, even if they have similar landscapes. In that sense, the third eye is unlimited. But yes, like the physical eye, it does have parameters, which in some sense have limits or benchmarks.

11

MULTIDIMENSIONAL ASPECTS OF NOW

This is Angel Raphael. It becomes less easy to live in a linear sense, even one dimensional in fifth or seventh or ninth dimension. Very tricky to try to walk a narrow path these days in terms of identity or efficiency or perception. In other words, to see things clearly in one slice, the way perhaps you used to feel you could judge politics or some situation as being good or bad or just specifically one thing. Now you might find the overlap, the bleed through, of different perspectives, is very hard to deny.

This is essentially what we mean about the multidimensional aspects of now. The more you can allow that there may be sensations, perceptions, interference even, from other dimensions, then you can sift through a bit better: "All right, what's happening right now?"

English-language audio of this following energy exercise is available available free online with the link at the end of the book.

To engage with this exercise through the words below, invite the angels to

65

participate with you using Angel Raphael's words as a focus. Pause in between lines or paragraphs to reflect or feel the energies.

ENERGY EXERCISE: AXIS POINTS

We do want to do an exercise with you to begin. This is Raphael. If you'd like to sit comfortably, easily, but also where your spine is erect—like garden hose without any kinks in it—so the energy can flow through easy, breezy.

We want to run some energy with you, starting from top of the spine. The very top inside the skull there, the top of the spine, and running down to the base of the spine. This conduit of energy is complete. Sometimes you look outside yourself for energy or information. We want to emphasize today that you are a complete conduit.

Yes, you can be connected with earth and sun, moon and stars and other individuals and trees, plants and animals, absolutely. And you are complete in your own conduit circuitry here. We're going to focus a moment on that, because some of you are feeling a little bit too much like you need to lean outside yourselves to feel completion or anchored, or upliftment.

All of those things, especially in the multidimensional now, are right within you, within your body self.

Focusing please on the top of the spine within the skull, going all the way down to tailbone or beneath bottom of the spine. You may feel some heat or energy or see some light or taste or smell something, depending on your ways of perceiving. Just putting your interest on these two points within your physical and energetic bodies: top of the spine, base of the spine.

You are aware, perhaps, that the Earth has an axis it rotates around. These points of the spine are your axis points. They show you where your rotation lies. When you move, you are anchored in to these pivot points. They don't move when you move. In other words, top of the spine doesn't move to the left shoulder. It stays in relation to you in the same place. These axis points are quite important.

When you are a conduit for multidimensional energy, it can be helpful to come back to these axis points if you feel a little lost. If you feel a little bit like there's so much going on in the energies: "I don't know whether to feel tired or wired or stressed or relieved—all of the above at once." Focusing a little bit on base of the spine, top of the spine, can help you to recognize where your axis points lie.

Because when you move interdimensionally, or experience and perceive interdimensionally, you are as you embodied (in a body), in an energy body as well. And yes, the soul is anchored in there, inhabiting, if you like, the body space—or perceiving through the body space might be more accurate. When you move interdimensionally, you bring these axis points of the spine with you. They are your reference, and they are your pillar.

And you pivot around those points.

Today, we're using focus on these two points as a kind of anchoring in remembrance: "Ah, this is who and what I am."

Yes, the energies are quite fluid and interesting and sometimes overwhelming, and perhaps you're a bit forgetful in some moments who and what you are. You can use these two reference points, anchor points, to bring you back into where you are and who you are within this multidimensional now. We're not speaking now of your ancestral multidimensional self or your future multidimensional self. But right now, as you experience the world if you feel a little bit lost or adrift, helpful to focus on top of the spine, base of the spine.

Just breathe into these points of you.

From these axis points, so many nerves run through blood vessels as well—oxygen, all of that—but primarily nervous system branches out from these points quite significantly. When you perceive—when you see, smell, touch, feel the earth beneath—it comes from the nervous system branches, roots, tendrils that come out of the spine in these two points significantly. Your roots and branches, if you like, come through here.

In other words, in this analogy, if you were in a forest of trees, and there was sun and light and a bunch of things going on, and wind, you could remember: "Oh, I have branches, I have roots. I am this tree. Yes, I'm interconnected with all beings in some sense. And yes, there are many, many points of stimuli. And I'm just here. I have roots and branches. I am."

Bringing your awareness back out into your outer perception of the world at this moment in the room or the outdoor environment you're in. Looking around a little or moving your shoulders a little. Something to bring yourself a bit back into the physical self. You can maintain that awareness, if you like, on the spine. That's not going to hurt, but we're coming out of this exercise.

This is Angel Ariel. It's an interesting moment when there's so much in transition, to know who and what you are, even though who and what you are does change. Like the tree, from the seed, essentially the empty or the void, to the fully sprouted plant and then tall tree that then creates new seeds. All of these are reference points, but you never lose who you are. At this moment, with such tremendous growth and change afoot for you personally, it's very good to anchor in a bit who you are right now. Not so much concerned about who you might be tomorrow or next month, next week. But who are you right now? And by <u>who</u>, we don't mean: What have you accomplished? What is your persona right now? but feeling: "What is my energy? Where am I?" That's what we mean by who. It's more of a sense of being than definition from anyone else from the outside.

. . .

68

Could you speak a little to the influence on our DNA which we have had? As I understand it, this is something that has affected me personally, and may have affected some others, about reptilian influence that it's perhaps shifting because of the incoming higher frequencies. What is shifting? And what's the impact on what has been, in a sense?

Adria: It's a great question, because I do feel like, personally and a few other people have mentioned too, that reptilian or a clearing of that is one of the first stages, or part of one of the first stages of this transition.

Absolutely. This is Raphael. To speak contextually here, first reptilian has been a dominant theme on the outer social sphere for, let's say, the last 100-300 years. In terms of what you came into this world with, the influences around you and within you, reptilian has been quite strong.

Now, many of you have matured out of seeing that as the only truth. For example, fear or anger as being the only responses to things, or "right" or justified responses to things, right? Many of you have grown out of that. Yet those impulses can still be there. The wave of anger. The wave of fear. Certainly in the way that society has been run, there is a lot of reptilian influence right now in terms of hierarchical structures and suppression, essentially, of free will and creative thought, creative being.

It's not that there hasn't been arts and leisure to some extent around the world, but this value on human productivity, particularly has been a sign of reptilian influence in the social sphere. That's what we would call unhealthy. Now if you're looking at harnessing the most use—as an external reptilian force—from humankind, maybe productivity is wonderful. We're just speaking from angelic value system. This idea that "the more that I can be awake and alert and producing something, then I have more value," that comes from the external reptilian view.

Now in the 12 sacred or pure or clinically-derived galactic strains of the new human DNA, reptilian is one of the 12. So you're not jettisoning reptilian and saying: "Oh, now I'm moving on to Pleiadian and other higher forms of consciousness. I can just leave this behind." However, in its pure sense as well, it does remain quite structural and knee-jerk reactions, let's say.

It's helpful to have those. It's helpful to not have to stop and think for 10 minutes or an hour when there's a wildfire. It's helpful to have knee-jerk reactions. And structure to some extent can be helpful. But we would suggest most of you will not live in your reptilian self very often, but have access to it. Anger or fighting back, for example, can also be quite healthy, even in a very high spiritual sense. Or a very practical sense, if you were defending a child from some attack or something like that. Helpful to be able to step in with a sort of violent protectiveness, something like that. Again, there's helpful aspects to the reptilian in you. We don't want you to feel you need to jettison that or move on to a whole of you that doesn't have that as a part. However, we would suggest it will be less used.

I *hadn't realized that such a high proportion of the influence on humanity was reptilian. I was aware of the reptilian brain, but I wasn't aware that it was such a big influence on the majority of humanity*

Yes. This is Raphael. Subjugation is one word there, one accurate description. It's not that reptilians don't have other value or heightened beauty that can add to your full divine expression of humankind—the 12 strains. But it's helpful right now for contrast to know: "Okay, some of this I am outgrowing or leaving behind, but some of it is going to remain part of me."

Some of you have had some clearings in that regard, around your more base instincts, and that's alright, just let it flow through. Good not to act on lower impulses. But to feel them is not a problem. You know, you may be clearing some of that, so not to be alarmed about that within yourself. Even, let's say, from an ego standpoint, a sudden tendency to want to be top of the heap. That might be a reptilian clearing—something in you is wanting to recognize or let go of how that's been the game. "Either I'm at the bottom of the heap or the top of the heap."

Something in your widening conscious field says: "Wait a minute. Are these the only options?" But sometimes it comes out in almost a cartoonish way, and you have a clearing of: "I want to finally be on top of the heap." And the other parts of you that are more mature can just witness that and say: "All right, but there might be other games we can play too." As long as you're not acting out from anger, violence, or fear, it's all right to feel them, and that may be part of the transmigration here of you. Good to be aware.

INTERNALIZED REPTILIAN JUDGEMENT

This is Angel Raphael. If you were to look at shame from the outside as an external judgment, the feeling is you're somehow an unpalatable type of creature. The reptilian view of humans, at least initially—now this will and does evolve, but let's say back historically to the era when humankind is first being born . . . Reptilians have this nice, protective skin layer. They are hardened to life. They have a certain strength to them. And humans came out looking soft and squishy and weird and unable to fend for themselves for so very long, and even then, they seem very weak, right?

If you look at shame from that angle, it's a perspective of judgment of: "There's something not right about these ill-formed weaklings." That's one viewpoint of humankind. And we're neutral to this. We can see also, yes, if you're a beetle with a hard shell and you look at a worm or something, they look vulnerable, exposed. And why would any creature live like that? There is a truth to that, so called truth.

When you are looking at all these different perspectives of yourself as a human (from the Pleiadian, reptilian and so on), there will be these moments where you see yourself, perhaps, oddly. Most will be positive or neutral. Reptilians tend to be more judgmental. It's in their nature. It's what has kept them alive. Again, that's a neutral quality; but they do have more judgment. This fierceness of anti-human largely is the natural judgment of reptilian to human. Because the reptilian strand is within you—it is one of the 12 galactic strands—you have internalized the viewpoint of yourself (of the whole human, or let's say, the old human, without these 12 activated) as something to be ashamed of, something that is wrong, something that's not quite good enough. Not right.

When you start with that as a default, it's very hard to ever catch up. Because you're not going to grow lizard skin. You're not going to become hardened rulers, hierarchical. And so you're never going to measure up to that standard. This is where the conscious self can say: "Oh, okay, I see why there's that viewpoint of me." And that's correct. It's to be ashamed of if you're thinking of measuring up to a certain dictatorial standard.

But if I want to look at the compassionate human heart or other standards, "maybe I think very well of myself. Or if I want to look at the Pleiadian knowledge perspective, or the Lyran music perspective, innovations in music from old humankind: "Wow, there's a marvel happening here—different harmonics and voice has technologically speaking, different capabilities than the Lyran physical self. Much to marvel at here." That's why the human voice is so potent for healing with music, other races don't necessarily have within them, they have instrumentation, but not necessarily within them.

It's certainly not all negative. Some people think: "Well, galactic beings are all higher. They all must be looking at 'little humans need to grow up.'" No, that's not the case. From many race standpoints, galactic race standpoints, human is an evolution or a betterment on what they physically have, or emotionally, or mentally, or compassionately have.

You do have this very strong—looking negatively at humanity—that's internalized from the reptilian and is reinforced because through long periods of human history, reptilians have been among the elites behind the scenes. Society has been reinforcing through that elite: "You should be ashamed. You should think badly, oddly of yourself." It's external and internal, so it runs very deep and over many generations.

What can we do to clear that?

With all of this positive and negative activation and clearing, it's witnessing with love. Yes, it's there. You could even acknowledge there's some truth to that, and that's helpful. Instead of trying to push back to the new different kind of, let's say, Dragon perspective, or the old kind of "this feels creepy or negative" perspective, accepting: "Yes, I see that. I see how that is one viewpoint" with love and then just letting it be.

Then you'll find what's naturally happening as your frequency is increasing is that those viewpoints that hold a higher density do fall away. They do clear naturally. You don't have to push them out. You don't have to feel: "I have to elbow this out. I have to strong arm it. I have to be so positive to get all the negative out!" That's an assertive approach. That's just not needed, because when you are oscillating at a higher frequency, these things shift out, almost like sand. So it happens quite naturally. And sometimes there's discomfort in that, because when something's shaking out, you see it. You see it fall out, and you think: "Uh oh, that's me." Or: "What's going on?"

Again, when things clear, they often look brightest or loudest. But it's clearing out. And that's part of the discernment. "Am I witnessing something that's coming alive in me that's new? Or am I witnessing what has been internalized? Now I'm just noticing it. And maybe I'll have a conscious choice to not let that rule me. And hopefully I'll evolve out of that as well and not have that impression so strongly in my psyche."

And that's the case with reptilian. The more dense, let's call them, aspects of the reptilian, they can't really coherently stay with you as you rise into these higher vibrations. And the other of the 12 activations (more or less) also increase your frequency. Reptilian in that sense, is a bit outnumbered in your frequency self. You really don't have to worry about pushing out or clearing that on your own. It's happening. It really doesn't stand a chance of sticking around for those of you who have chosen to remain in the higher frequencies and not just notice them for a minute and shut them down and step back to the old way. Because that's still a choice for everyone, each human on the planet.

This is, as many have said, an embodiment of higher frequencies. It's not about conceptual or contextual awareness, or being in meditation, where you levitate up out of your body and feel that you're in the bliss field. You are embodying all of these changes. The heart is like the director, like the movie director and the script writer as well—writer/director—they set the direction. But then the body is part of the acting that out in the world and living that in the sense of vibratory aliveness.

At different stages of this, you will feel the womb, gut, lungs, skin, many parts of yourself, not just say, third eye, activating in a very real, tangible sense. And the mind really doesn't need to keep track or direct, because, again, the mind is not the director here; the heart is. The heart just says: "What I want," for example, "is for all of these 12 galactic strains to really activate in me, even the reptilian. So I have the full knowledge base. I have the full skill set. And then I can pick and choose what I want."

When we say activating the reptilian, the purity of the intent was to share what is right about the DNA. What we have just spoken about is some of the negative layering that came with the, let's say, interracial feelings. That's different. It is important for the reptilian to be active in you, so that you have it as a functional part that you can turn on and off, or listen to, or decide: "No, that's not so important in my daily life, but I'm glad I have that fight or flight response" or whatever it is, or "the ability to be cold and stern when needed." You may not use it very much, but it's helpful to have your whole skill set.

RECEIVING CHANGE

I just was wondering the feeling of being adrift, I guess, sort of unfocused without purpose, is that to do with all the changes that are coming in the multidimensionality? I feel not part of life, and I'm just wondering if that is part of all this new DNA coming online and all those changes that we're going through?

This is Raphael. This is a one-dimensional aspect of yourself that is letting go of the need to define. We'll speak a little bit about this, because it's showing up or hitting each of you in slightly different ways here, and can be helpful to understand what this is, why in some of you it feels adrift, in some of you there's a sense of frustration, but not really attached to anything, any outer circumstance. And certainly the sense of disconnect.

When you jump fully into the 12-dimensional self, but 12-dimensional self isn't quite online yet fully, and yet to really begin that process, you do essentially leave behind your old ways of viewing the world. In the meantime, even though you're moving from what was very defined, almost one-dimensional view of the world to multi layered, multidimensional view, in the meantime, you're almost both and neither. That can feel quite adrift. And disorientation can occur.

An important thing to notice here is nothing has gone wrong, from angelic perspective. If you're feeling these feelings, may not be just this month. It may be here and there across a transition, you may down the road, have seven of your galactic strains activated, and you're feeling them and enjoying and then one day, one month, you just feel again, like, whoa. I don't feel connected to any of this. That's quite, quite natural.

You really are inhabiting a new world. It's your world. It's one that you have created and/or have co-created with, along with others, and yet it is so new. If any of you have had jet lag or culture shock when you move somewhere, or you visit for a long time, it doesn't happen right away, that you feel so disoriented. It's usually some months or weeks down the road, all of the sudden, there's part of you that rebels, essentially. "Wait a minute! This isn't the familiar place, and I don't understand. So I'm going to be mad about it." Essentially, this is how it plays out in culture shock. Even though you're excited to live in this new land or visit for some months, some part of you that wants the familiar rebels. "Wait a minute! Where is my breakfast the way I like it? Why is the sunlight different here? Why do people speak funny? I'm just going to be mad about it"

This is not reptilian, but it is, let's say, a mammalian or less mature response. But it's quite natural when you are evolving into something new to have some stages where you essentially, energetically or emotionally, are crossing your arms saying: "Hmph! I don't like this! Where is everything the way it's supposed to be?"

Because to visit, let's say two weeks or a month somewhere, is all right. But when you're going to reside there, and it's a foreign land, then these kind of responses kick in. So many of you are experiencing that now, again, quite natural.

One thing you can do is rely on comfort food of many kinds—books that you like to read, foods or sensations or smells or walks that are familiar. In other words, it's not that you can exactly stop growing, but you can put a little less emphasis on the transformation for a while. It's not going to slow down what's going on, but you might want to be more earthy, more practical, more simple for a little while.

Whether it's fun things or cleaning the house or just standing out on the earth and just the simplicity of knowing where I am who I am. That's why we started with this exercise today with the spine. Not needing to in these moments, burst forward into brand new, creative sparks and transformations, because that is happening at such a rate, and it's happening collectively at such a rate that it is all right to essentially slow down or even go back. It's not that you're going to un-transform, but what you would consider perhaps lower vibratory music or entertainments or foods, or just less meditation for an hour a week or a month, not pushing so much towards the transformative edge and looking for areas of comfort for yourself. That's what we would suggest. You're not going to again, stop transforming or go backwards. But sometimes, to go back to culture shock, what helps the most is to recognize it for what it is, but then maybe smell a familiar smell, or have that candy bar from home or something that just feels like "Okay, okay." There's some reference points.

It does not have to be lower vibratory, but you want to look for some comfortable reference points that don't require growth and stretching and transformation so much. Allowing yourself, especially if that's where your passions lie in this life moving forward that there may be some weeks—not months, we would say—but there may be some weeks at a time where you really want to slow down and give yourself permission not to do that. Because it's happening anyway within you.

You're not going to un-transform or un-ascend. But if there's something in you that's saying: "Hold on, I just want to slow down." It's all right to essentially give yourself that, and that's what we would recommend. In any child or any plant or any cerebral or emotional project, there are growth spurts, and then there's moments to catch up with all of that. Although this is still a very highly energized time, you may be finding <u>because</u> of that, that you need to slow down in some other aspects when you're able.

. . .

*W*hat sort of physical changes can we expect? I mean, I've been quite nauseous for the last few days, and it doesn't feel like my own body, somehow. I don't know how to say that. Maybe it's the Earth energy. Maybe it has something to do with these changes? That would be my question, the physical changes that come with this whole thing.

Yes. This is Raphael. Again here, comfort is helpful, whether that's a warm bath or certain foods. Even if you think: "Well, this isn't on my new diet." It can help.

We'll rely on science fiction here for a moment, which is often based in fact. If you have seen any of these transformations for X-Men, comic books or movies, something like that, it is not unusual for the creature that is being transformed, who will be the superhero, but is currently in the first transformations, to be screaming in pain or feeling some shock or disorientation or not liking what's happening and certainly not understanding what's happening.

Physically, physiologically, there is quite a lot going on. To move from a two-strand DNA to a 12-strand DNA system is a lot physically. When you have activations—solar and other galactic light activations —it provokes this change in you, whether you want it or not.

It's not necessarily that you're nauseous because you sat down and meditated for 12 hours. Could have been a sun spurt or some other frequency. Maybe there's a group meditating on Earth, and they raise the frequency, and so now your transformations start heating up and getting active more quickly. There can be a lot of external factors why suddenly your body just essentially feels unwell, freaks out a little.

We would say nothing's going wrong. You're not doing it wrong. You're not transforming incorrectly. And it's not that you just have to eat some green algae and then you'll be all right. Sometimes there are periods of discomfort with this kind of transformation, absolutely— emotional, physical, all of the above. To look: "Where can I step things back a little? Maybe I can't tell the sun not to be sending me so much solar wind this hour. But if I had planned on chanting for four hours or reading a spiritual text. Maybe, is there something I can do that's less activating or transforming right now?"

Again, not that you want to go into violence or stepping backwards in your transition, and you really cannot do either of those things at this stage, but understanding it may be time to sit back a little on the other parts of the transformation. Let's say you were listening to repeats of some of these exercises or things like that, when you already feel nauseous. "Okay, maybe I better slow things down a little." Have some comfort food, have a bath, take a gentle walk outside, something that is not going to provoke more high cellular movement.

But the short answer is, all of this is to be expected, not denied in yourself. But also not to crush down on yourself with disappointments or regret that things are not high functioning in terms of, again, the reptilian sense of value of productivity. Can you imagine, in these comic books or movies strips, that while the creature was becoming a weather machine or a werewolf or whatever it was, right in that moment, someone said to them: "Why are you late on your accounting files?" Or "You didn't do your 10 hours of shoveling," or whatever it was. And yet, you do.

We see many humans putting themselves in this boat of compare and contrast. "Well, last week or last month, I got all these things done, and now I just feel nauseous and I'm not getting anything done." That is a reptilian kind of judgment from the exterior. Are you being productive or not? Instead, you might ask yourself very gently: "Is there a transformation going on? And if so, is it going right? Or does it need something of me?" Sometimes there is a physical component, like exercise or some vitamin or mineral that can help. Or: "Do I just need to understand this is what's going on right now? This is the headline news." And to let it be.

. . .

79

Some say that we will have three days of darkness. I'm just wondering a little bit about that and how this also fits together?

This is Angel Raphael. Both are true. For all of you who are listening live now, you have opted to be early in your transitions. As we've been saying since about 2019, the energies are open, already—fully open. The whole spectrum of frequencies that you would need for all these transformations is already there. And so many of you are already jumping in to transform on a cellular level. However, there will be predictably—so this can change, but we would say in the forecast—it looks like there will be a big galactic light event and blackout of technologies on Earth for some days as a result.

When you say darkness, it may not be literally that the sun goes out, but it may be darkness in. technological sense. There will be the seed moment for many who have been waiting to collectively experience the ignition of the change. But each of you listening now, today are already in this change. So it's a little bit of both/and. You may also experience even more uplift at that time when there's a big wave of galactic light that comes in.

This is highly positive from our vantage point. It's not like a meteor hitting Earth, and then all is lost. But you've already seen with some of the high solar Earth's sun light, that high frequency light hitting Earth has some disruptive effects on your physical self and also on technologies. So this, we would say, predictably again, could change. But it looks like it's still on track to happen. A massive light like that, a short term massive light, and then some days of technological blackout as a result. This will be the ignition for many to begin this change that you're already in, the cellular change. So you don't have to wait for that, and you don't certainly, from angelic perspective, need to fear it. It is welcome conditions for the massive transformation of many thousands on Earth, thousands of humans.

. . .

When you say solar light, are you also, are you talking about the photonic light that has come to all of us during this period of time? I think of it like everybody's frequency is rising because of that. Maybe that's more of a steady thing that's been happening, and not like a big event?

This is Raphael. Yes, that's been very active in the last more than one year now. Frequently, not every day, but frequently, more bursts of we're speaking now of the Earth's sun. The big three days of darkness is projected as solar light from another earth's sun coming through in a big way. Galactic light, you could call it, or still solar light, but not the Earth's sun that you've become used to. And yes, it's available to all, but you've seen as in this last year, not everyone makes use of it for ascension. Some people just feel the frustration that their GPS is off for a while, or don't feel anything at all. So not everyone is signing up to use this light for their own ascension, but it's available for everyone, and certainly collectively there's an uplift occurring.

Does it have anything to do with if the crown chakra is open or not to receive the light?

Yes and not yes. This is Raphael. If you know that you want to ascend, you don't necessarily have to know what that means, technically speaking, technologically speaking. You don't have to worry: "Do I have to prepare by opening a certain chakra or saying certain mantras or doing particular type of food or exercise or spiritual practice?" Because there are so many ways of support and so many outlets for this light once it's active in you.

Open chakras of all kinds—heart, crown, root—are helpful. But you can also know that that will happen on its own when it needs to. The same way that a flower will open when the sun conditions are right. You don't have to go pry it open, right? It just happens. So you don't need to be concerned that there's something you need to do to prepare. It really is more about the intent. Do I want to receive this and transform or not?

～

English-language audio of this following energy exercise is available available free online with the link at the end of the book.

To engage with this exercise through the words below, invite the angels to participate with you using Angel Raphael's words as a focus. Pause in between lines or paragraphs to reflect or feel the energies.

ENERGY EXERCISE: ANCHOR POINTS

This is Raphael. We'll have a little bit of an exercise now to integrate all this.

Coming again to the points of light at the top and the base of your spine, and noticing that they are and do connect, but not always. In other words, you have a base of the spine. You have a top of the spine. Not all of the neurological impulses are running all of the time, running hot all of the time. You're not getting stimulus from all of your roots and branches all of the time, or your system would burn out, burn too bright, right? Trusting that although this is there—those anchor points—the energy will run along the nervous system conduits when it needs to.

In the meantime, it's good enough, well enough to know you have these anchor points and that you're in a time of great change. So not to force that everything needs to be lit up all at once right now, and that you either have to be fully functional in the old way, or fully functional in the new way. To allow that you're in a transit time now please, and have compassion with yourself. However this shows up for you.

Welcoming in yourself that you are being in transition.

Maybe time for an hour or a moment, not to have so much light running along this conduit of the spine. Yet it's healthy. All the conduits are there, the axis points are there—base and crown.

All is as it should be. All is right with your transforming self.

Giving yourself that blessing of compassion, right now. "I am a multidimensional self with a lot going on. It's alright to expect less, in an outward sense, during such a transformative time."

No one else is going to give you permission or withhold permission. You can just gift that to yourself right now, please.

Watch how the universe bends and shapes to allow what you have allowed in yourself. If it's less working, look how less work is demanded from the outside. Certain types of rest or calibration, how that shows up. You give yourself permission for that, and the universe will comply. Needs to start with you.

Beautiful. Thank you all for being so brave to transform and to be so conscious to transform with grace and self-love.

You are where you are right now, and that's the right place to be. We're speaking about your energy, your way of being—the right place to be.

12

LEARNING TO FLY AGAIN

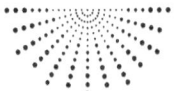

This is Angel Raphael. Each of you, in various methods, lives and know-hows, have flown in many different avenues— physically, intellectually, metaphysically, most certainly. We'll speak about a few different aspects of flight, some quite literal. We'll start with that sense of limitation and belief, as you have crafted into your adulthood, the understanding of what the body can and cannot do.

The body cannot fly (human body). That's obvious, evident, right? A body has so many toes, generally five, not four toes. You have this nose which can smell and so on. You've just learned about yourself, and that has not felt like limitation. It's felt like knowing what the body is capable of and being sensible and aware.

And yet, when you come into your 12-dimensional being, all the aspects of you, you can, in fact, fly, quite literally. Some of this will play out in different dimensions, and some in the one that your body is most typically in (fifth or seventh for most of you). It's not that this is necessarily visible to all, but in some cases, yes. In some cases, it will look, perhaps in other dimensions, like you have wings. In some cases, it will look to those viewing from third or fifth that you just hopped a little or levitated. It will be interesting to see the feedback you get as you move into this flight, who can see and who cannot see. It starts with you and your own direct experience.

Now, what is the reason for flight? You might just say: "What is the reason for seeing or walking?" It just is. It's not from angelic vantage point, a higher state of being. It's just that when you are practically aware of what the human can and cannot do, and you've put flying in the can't do category without some kind of apparatus or airplane, we'd like you to put it back in the can do, or learning how to again. Because in other life expressions, and for some of you, in your dream space and so on, and you have flown already.

Read through the meditation below first, then close your eyes to melt into the experience.

MEDITATION: EXPERIENCE OF FLIGHT

We'd like to take you in a meditative, explorative sense here, first, into the experience of flight and what it feels to be weightless, in the sense that gravity is not responsible for pinning you down to Earth. You have other options.

If you'd like to close your eyes and just feel right now in your energetic field, more than the physical self, if there feels like there is resistance or pressure, such as gravity. Or if it feels like there is a buoyancy. Not trying to change it right now, just noticing what it feels like.

If you like, one way in is, what does the air feel like around you? Does it feel like it is pressing into you, or holding you up?

We're going to ask your energetic self, because you have traveled a few times now interdimensionally—some of you much more than that—to move into a dimension where the environment supports flight and floating. Still with the eyes closed, inviting yourself to shift into one of the dimensions—there are several—where flight and buoyancy is quite easy. As you do so, feel if the air around you shifts at all.

Begin to get a sense if you have wings in this dimension, or if it's more of a floating reality.

Perhaps, it feels quite normal, but in that dimensional sense, look around and notice, are you in fact in the sky?

Remembering to breathe and soothe any sense of self that feels alarmed in any way. It's all right. We're just exploring a bit. We'll come back to what is known. Feeling the sensation of the air around yourself. If you are visually inclined, what does it look like around you in this dimension that supports flight or floating?

Do you have wings or are you riding currents of air?

Anything else you notice from a sensory perspective.

Very gently at your own time, bringing yourself into the dimension you started out reading this in—may be fifth or something similar.

Carrying with you the remembrance of the other dimension, but pulling yourself gently back into this one from a functional perspective.

This is Angel Raphael. How is it possible that you might have wings but you might not in that dimension, and still you can float or fly? In the 12-dimensional self, strictly speaking—now there are other methods of flight, but we'll stick with that today—the angelic is one of the flight mechanisms. Some of you experienced going there.

Dragon also can float or fly with or without wings. There are different types of dragon-selves. If you have seen Chinese depictions

87

of dragon, sometimes they're quite lean and long, and wings may be small or not there at all, and yet those creatures are in the air, space. Some dragons you have seen depictions of with quite large wings. Both of those are galactic archetypes. You have likely chosen one or the other, and not both, in terms of what you are in your imprint DNA-self.

Now, there are other creatures who have flight. Fairies, for example. Fairies are not one of the 12 galactic imprints in the new human DNA. You may see and notice fairies and be quite friendly with them. Doesn't mean that you are one. If you are, that is another part of yourself, and not the human 12th-dimensional expression we speak of.

All things are possible. We don't mean to limit with our descriptions, but to help tailor what you might have some feeling inkling of, of what to look for or notice. Because most likely, you won't be in a dragon-self and an angelic-self at the same hour at the same timeprint. So you can feel around with your different senses, if any of them are active, which of those feels right at that time? It also is not important to know with the mind. You might just have noticed if there was a different sensation of the air around you, or there were any other impressions, when you traveled to one of the dimensions of flight.

There is a buoyancy, a lightness around you that now, when you are listening from the dimension you are in. You might feel a little spacious, ungrounded. Angels, for example, do not have gravity in the same sense of what you have been born into. That's how they can be in multiple places around the world and fly so high and so low without any issue. There's a buoyancy, a weightlessness, a wonder, to that, as long as you're not trying to contrast it with the human of your adult-self before 12-dimensional up-rising.

Because if you contrast it, then it feels a bit too light, right? It feels like: "Where's the ground?" Now, the dragon flight, although it may have more a sense of drift or buoyancy, also has a largess to it. Dragon bodies are typically much larger than the angelic, and again, have a different dimensional density, frequency. Still quite a lot of shimmer and magic. Dragons, depending on, again, your affinity there, may be much, much more akin to water, sky, earth. Most dragons do have flight.

You're not expected to explore all of those right now. But we want you to playfully practice when you feel like it, leaning into those flightier dimensions, especially when the world feels too heavy in terms of the physical pains or suffering in the emotional body or mental angst about what's going on in society or politics. You might too, with our permission, use one of the flying dimensions as an escape route or a rest.

Even those of you who work very hard for the most part believe in sleep, or rest, or pausing for a meal. It's not that you're going to escape the pains of the body or politics, but to learn that you have options. When it feels like you could use some light or lightness or buoyancy, it's good to rest into that sense of flight. So right now, first journey, maybe you're not flying halfway across the Earth in the same physical vessel you're reading these words in. However you might, by the end of this year, be doing so.

For now, it's helpful to lean into the sense of: Does the air itself, the supporting environment, feel different when you're in a dimension of flight? And can you notice that there are parts of you that are weightless and don't have gravitational pull?

The more you play with different sensations like this, the less alarming it will feel when they come in suddenly. Because the way your intuition does, some of the dimensional awarenesses are going to start to tug at you at various times in order to let you know: "Hey, I have something to offer here." Or "Hey, this dimensional self, or this dimension is the best place to go right now for what you're feeling, grieving, imagining, co-creating, enjoying, enlightening into . . .

In a very instinctual way, you're going to be moving into these different dimensions, and different parts of yourself are going to tug at you a bit. If you were feeling very grounded, and then all of a sudden you felt flighty, spacious, if you've been practicing just for fun, leaning into those dimensions of flight, it may not cause so much panic or alarm. It might just be like: "Oh, I wonder if the angelic or the dragon in me is trying to get out to say something or share some of its gifts? Or perhaps there is a being in one of those dimensions that's calling for my attention, has something to say or to gift."

Much of this in these early days, weeks and years, experiences of beings in different dimensions is going to be around friendship and gifts and sharing messages and knowledge. There might feel there's an urgency or a tug, not because your house is on fire, but because a friend is nearby and trying to gift you a clue about how you might get what is you just said you wanted, or how they might want to come visit your Earth, your version of Earth, and so on.

It's quite playful and quite collaborative here, this 12-dimensional reality, even though at the core of it, we're speaking about you and your aspects of self, different dimensional aspects of self. What that opens for you is many, many different worlds of other types of beings and your collaborative possibilities there to just receive messages, or gifts, or understanding, or friendship. This is not from our vantage point about saving the world or saving you, saving anything. It's about tremendous expansion. The gift of being a new type of human.

Read through the meditation below first, then close your eyes to experience.

MEDITATION: SENSATIONS OF FLIGHT

We're going to travel again together here. This is Raphael. If you'd like to, closed eyes would be simpler for this, because it's more about the sensation of flight or feeling. If you felt you went to one, let's say angelic, and you want to go to the other, let's say dragon, you can guide that with your intent. If you're really not sure at all if you went anywhere or where you went, you could just ask for a different experience of flight in yourself.

Any sensations that arise, visual movies or sensations of the skin or smell or touch, just receive them. You don't have to do anything about it right now.

Linger, if you like. If you feel this other dimensional aspect tiring, you can just gently, very gently, slowly bring yourself back. It's up to you if you want to linger a bit longer or begin to come back.

Asking for the grace of integration. And here we offer this angelic support as well, let what you experience and know now be smoothly, swiftly integrated into your understanding of self.

When you're ready, coming back to the sense of presence the body-self that is reading this.

You are all of these. This is Raphael. It's not that you have to be so distinct to try to parse out in any given hour: "here am I in my more obviously human aspect or dragon or angel?" Because human does encompass all. Human in this case is the wider view; it includes all 12. There's not a separate human strand. But you might contrast it to the humanity of a few years back.

In other words, you're allowed to be all of these aspects all at once. And you are. So you don't have to worry so much about shutting the door between dimensions or shifting gears to be fully, fully back in your present-day self. Right now, it's more about feeling what do the different aspects of you feel like?

Cataloging a little bit for yourself, remembering what it was you just experienced, does help the mind. As we said before, the mind loves to categorize and catalog things. And so it helps the mental sense of fear or fear not when you take these mini explorations and notice, catalog what you noticed.

We don't mean you have to write it down or have a numbering system. We have shied away from giving these dimensions numbers in order to not have the mind be overly involved and concerned with hierarchy right now. Because it's much more of a wheel than a ladder —the dimensional realities.

When you have some clues, you may refine or change your mind about them later. That's all right. Don't worry about mis-categorizing. But if you had any sense of sensation or visual sense, or heart sense, or sense of knowing that was new to you, more expansive, perhaps, you can let the mind notice that a little, sift through, so that when it feels those sensations in everyday life, it doesn't panic about something that might be "wrong" with mental acuity or physical health.

That was interesting doing those exercises. On the first one, I did have an impression, although it wasn't super vivid, so I tend to think maybe it was just my imagination. But then, oftentimes the angels are like: "No, that was real." I just had this feeling of, I can't remember what the shape's called. It's like a donut that's like, kind of turning in on itself.

Adria: toroidal field?

Yeah. I had that same sensation once with the meditation on the heart guided by the angels. But I've always seen it going up from the heart space. And this time, for some reason, I just like felt it going the other way, and there's almost some kind of like propulsion going, like pushing me up, which is kind of interesting.

And then on the second one, I just got this really floating feeling almost. It's like as if you're falling on a roller coaster or something like that. I was like: Oh, you know what? This is kind of similar to how I feel when I'm really excited or happy, or like, just came off the stage after performing music or something. That's maybe what they're talking about, bringing it in? Or how connecting with that extra dimensional *like flying feelings and whatnot could practically help, if you could just put yourself in that mood or that floaty feeling consciously or purposefully. Maybe that would help in navigating life or something. Maybe the angels could speak on that.*

This is Raphael. To speak about the heart for a moment, we had the exercise where we showed the 12 dimensional lines coming through the belly button. And we have spoken quite a lot about the heart as your director's chair or the hub. There is also a command center there that controls, dimensionally, where you are. It does look like that from a certain vantage point, that the circulatory system energetically can change the field there, around the heart in different directions and shapes. That is essentially what bends the dimensions or allows you to shift.

You were seeing something quite literal. Although it's not necessary to pictorially view it that way in order to shift dimensions. For those of you who can perceive or see that something is different around the heart field, yes, when you shift dimensions, the field there palpably shifts like currents in the ocean or tides going in and out. It looks like it is the same, but not quite the same. Yes, absolutely.

In terms of buoyancy, emotional buoyancy, let's take one thread of what you spoke about—performing. Yes, you will learn to be able to bring in some of these qualities from the other dimensions, so that you're not so beholden anymore to depression, anger and so on. Because it's like adding spice to a recipe, you can quickly shift the alchemical reaction by bringing in some of the other seasonings from the other dimensions. In other words, the other aspects of yourself to balance out.

It's not that you're going to run from "reality." Like: "Well, I said some harsh words, and someone was sad, and so I feel badly about that. Oh, I better put in the happy juice." No, it's not that you're going to run from life and its consequences, but sometimes you feel the suppression or repression of the whole of society or someone else in your home, and you just want to take some ownership for your own well-being. The other dimensional parts of you can help with that. Yes, you'll be able to access that buoyancy of just after performing without necessarily being in that circumstance. It's a good example.

Yeah, thanks a lot. Glad they brought it around to that practicalness of, the usefulness of bringing that in. Because I've thought since they first brought it up about trying to physically fly, and I've been hearing a lot of stories that happening, mostly children. Honestly for me, I still have major doubts that, even if I tried in this lifetime, for a long time, that I actually could accomplish it.

Raphael: We would encourage for you and others who think: "Well, this is crazy!" Or: "Well, it's not crazy for that person. But I won't be able to," or something along those lines, to approach it with a question mark. "Well, what if? What if there is something very tangible to this flight? Or maybe for me, it's more of a sensation or lightness in my ability to navigate life."

If you just have a gentle question mark. We're not asking to make a religion around this, that people should fly, and you're a better person if you fly, and this is your birthright and all of that. We're making light of that. In different scenarios those kinds of statements are very important, but not in this one. We just are opening the possibility so that you can explore and experiment.

Even when you fly, you might not like it, so it doesn't mean you have to continue to fly, but it's nice to know that there's at least an open question that might have changed.

The exercises seem to bring back memories of ancient Egypt and the avian people.

This is Raphael. Some of the depictions in different places around the world, on caves, in the pyramids, sometimes modern scientists have interpreted: "Well that person that had wings, that must have been a sign of a tribe—avian tribe--or something. You know, it must have been a religious, spiritual, cultural belief." But sometimes it's quite literal.

Some of you have memories of other times and places on this Earth. This is not the only answer to this question, but part of what has happened at different timeprints on Earth. Let's say one of your 12 galactic strands, the galactic race representing that strand was here on Earth, historically practicing their gifts. Some of them had flight or had different color skin, and so that's depicted. It becomes part of the iconography of different religious cultural practice. But at that time, in many cases, it was quite literal and it was galactic. And so then you moving into your new 12-dimensional self, have aspects of some, not all, but some of those galactic fields and races.

It's a wonderful time to experience. "Oh, my goodness, this is literal. And it's in me. I always thought that was an analogy or a metaphor." Much of it is quite literal. But again, doesn't mean that you have to get there in order to be whole or enlightened or to experience your best life. But there's so much more to you now, and will continue to be so in the coming year, as you unfold into this.

Can you speak just for a moment about comparisons between experiences?

This is Raphael. You're not all exploring the same dimension at the same while. When we do these exercises, so important not to compare contrast too much with what others are feeling, or the perception or the interpretation of the perception. It's more important from angelic perspective that you maybe just notice "there was a sensation, or there was a little bit of a visual sense here." And just notice the clues.

. . .

95

I found the second time more like dragon energy. It started heavier and took longer to get flying, and the body position felt different.

Adria: Yeah, for me too, I felt dragon in the second one, and it was the sense of mass of the body, of the big kind of dragon for me. Definitely a weighty feeling in contrast to the angelic, which was more like floating around. Didn't really have so much of a body sense with that one.

This is Raphael. Interestingly, dragon can be used as a form of grounding, even when it's a dragon in flight. So as you are navigating tasks, and most importantly, perception, you can start to call on these different modes of being.

What of the 12 aspects of myself do I know might be able to take a certain mass (density mass) viewpoint on this? And give me information about how this hits in terms of visceral Earth? And that might be dragon. Or: "What of me might be able to literally rise above and not feel so weighted down by this time right now, and give more perspective?" And that might be angelic.

This will start to come through in your values and your knowledge of things. Early on, when we asked you this question: "What do I know?" It was, perhaps, at that time, more from a sense of intuition or inner self knowing. Now that question becomes so alive. What do I know? "Well, the dragon part of me knows what this feels like and the space it takes up in the physical world. And the angelic part of me knows how to see without limitation the vast picture of this and not feel limited by it," and so on through the 12. You get to have a much more nuanced perspective of knowledge as well.

As much as it is fun and very real that these are visceral experiences and physical ones, ultimately, it's more about your ability to perceive and receive information and to grow, to create your world and your understanding. All of this might seem quite fanciful, and that's all right. You don't have to take our word for it.

Also understand where we're headed is not so much about mystical magical lands with different creatures—although that literally is the case—but then what? What do you do with the interplay of this—that part of you are these different types of mystical, magical beings? How do you utilize that into your wholeness of self and expression and service and enjoyment and love? That's really where this is taking humankind. It's not so much about the Sci Fi or the fantasy movie. Yes, it will be. And for many of you, it will be that visceral and alive and real. But even beyond that, once that becomes "normal," you begin to notice how that changed your awareness of life and your ability to conceive of and perceive different viewpoints. And to create a marvelous New Earth. So New Earth has a lot to do with: What do we do with these gifts we're given?

13

MOVING BEYOND FIFTH DIMENSION TO A HUB EXPERIENCE OF ALL 12

This is Angel Raphael. In the coming years, we'll be speaking a lot, not just about fifth, but about the 12-dimensional experience. Moving from third to fifth as a platform or a base was necessary and vital to free yourself from the constraints of time and space in the way you've known them to be: it takes so long to get from here to there, or to accomplish something, or to achieve my goal. Or even to receive—in many cases that it will come in drips and drabs and not the treasure chest all at once.

Twelve-dimensional experience means you can be drawing from the gifts, the knowledge, the perceptive ability of these galactic lineages, both within yourself and outside of yourself, all at once. So you can see that things accelerate, either interdimensional learning, interdimensional exchange with others and/or your own gifts.

The inner would be your own expression of, let's say we've talked about the dragon and the angel, the Pleiadian, so far. The outer would be actually a dragon interdimensionally in your yard that you're having a telepathic conversation with. And so both. It's inner and outer of these 12 dimensions.

To the extent that you are able to relax control of needing it to be a certain way, because without really meaning to, perhaps you have very fixed idea about what is an angel, what is a dragon based on television, or children's stories, or something like that. In some cases, the truth may hit very close to that mark. And in some cases, very far, which could be disorienting for your brain, even though you know: "Well, maybe I shouldn't really be thinking basing it all on a Disney story, but this looks different (or the color is not right, or the accent, the tone of the language, is not what I expected)."

It does take an open mind not to hold what you thought of as fantasy realms, to a strict sense of your growing up—how you fixed them in your imagining.

Now, some of you do have remembrances from these other realms, from other lives or perhaps your childhood in this one, when the world felt more porous and there wasn't anyone telling you: "No, that's not what you should do." Or: "That's not truthful what you see in the yard."

But again, for the adult humans and the children now, things are wide open. So you may begin to catch glimpses and not yet know what it is that you see, or to hear things, or to know things and not understand. "Where does this come from? Is it from a new being on my guidance team? Is it from a friend trying to communicate with me—a galactic being in my yard, so to speak, or my home? Or is it my own sense of knowing unlocked from these lineages?"

The lineages, again, are not from past life experience. A galactic lineage is in the purity of the DNA itself. How does a dragon see and learn? What does it know? How do angels move? All of that becomes accessible to you.

You are a being of light, as are angels. You have more density or lower vibratory field as well, which shows up visually as a body-self, and in a felt sense, like you can touch yourself. It feels more dense than if you were to touch the angelic with your physical hand. And yet, you are also a being of light. If you were to look at yourself from a certain vantage point you're oscillating with color and light. How the angelic sees how and what you are is a loosely fitting shape of light. You come to think of yourself as this very dense container. Fingers and toes don't seem to change very much. Maybe they age, but they seem to be hard and fast, fixed as what they are. And yet you are light. And both are true.

Exploring these 12-dimensional aspects with your body-self as the hub. The senses are the hub of the experience, both inner and outer. We're going to include what you know in this also as a type of sense (sensory knowledge), because what you know is sometimes built out of perception of how you have seen or heard things, how you feel them to be. And sometimes it is more intangible than that, but it does still come from a sensory experience, even if you're not yet quite aware of how the knowing comes in, if it wasn't something you smelled or tasted or so on. How do you know that you're not going to like that—that your body is going to reject that particular plant, or herb, or food, or medicine? something in you knows, without even smelling inside the jar or tasting that plant. It is a type of sense, this knowing. you'll come to understand that as you open up more to yourself as this hub experience.

The beauty of being at the hub means you don't have to lose who and what you are. So in order to experience your lineage—as Dragon, Angel, Pleiadian and so on—you don't have to lose who your own childhood expression, your sense of self in terms of: who I want to be in the world, what I want to offer, what my preferences are.

But of course, those are going to change. When you travel to Europe, if you're coming from Latin America or vice versa, you change just from your two-week or two-month stay—talking to different people, hearing different accents, tasting different spices, seeing different viewpoints in nature. It changes you. You're never the same after that two-week or two-month voyage, in ways that perhaps you don't understand. Similarly, these other perspectives and the journeys you take interdimensionally change who you are, because they expand your sense of self and what's possible in the universe. "Where do I fit in all of this?"

At the same time, you are the hub. You are the transit point, so you don't have to worry about losing your way. You come back again and again through the senses to the heart space—the heart field, the toroidal field. That's what's collecting the light of you. And this electromagnetic push/pull that has its own sustainable wavelength of you. So you don't have to "keep it together," your light. You're not trying to hold it in, right? It's moving. It emanates, oscillates <u>from</u> you.

That is the container through which you travel. A container through which you bring back memory and shared expression A container through which you share into the quantum your own experience of life. Without meaning to, without writing a book or sharing a blog, necessarily, you're sharing your lived world with others through this electromagnetic pulse into the universe. This is also where you travel through and how you open and widen your senses of expression.

Because it's coming largely (not exclusively, but largely) through the toroidal field of the heart, you don't have that conflict that would happen if all of this was happening through the mind—the brain space. If it was happening through the mind, you're going to try to choose a primary identity of the 12, and you're going to try to make sense of the incongruities between the different ways of perceiving. But it's happening through the heart. It's a little bit like a field of, a meadow of, wild flowers. You don't try to make the yellow ones like the red or the purple ones that are tall, like the white ones that are small. You have the capacity to see them all. You might have favorites, but there's no sense of "Hmm, if I don't make all of these flowers look the same, then I'm losing my mind."

If all of this travel and new sensory expression was happening through the mind <u>primarily</u>, as third dimension <u>was</u>, you would get this sense of psychotic break most likely. That's the most frequent outcome when you try to do too much through the lens of the mind.

Because the mind wants things to be categorically the same, to be safe based on past expression and predictable.

The heart is a little more like a river. If it encounters a rock, it might take time to shape that rock, but it will. It will get its way. And if it encounters a rock and right now has somewhere to go, it just goes around. The mind would encounter a rock and think "I'm stuck here." And it might stay there staring at the rock for 20 years. You've all had something like that in your life. Because it doesn't occur to the mind: "I could go around, or just choose another path, do something different."

Water, which is much closer to your true nature now—more of a fifth-dimensional hub nature that's experiencing 12—knows how to evaporate, rain down again, be a slow, meandering stream, be a rushing river, be a tremendous ocean which is churning up earth and creating new island vistas, different landscapes through the force of its own nature. Of course, in this analogy, there are other things at play, the wind and the sun and so on. But to be clear here, you're just much more fluid. You're not so fixed as you imagine.

Yet you get to have the sanity, the sameness, of a body shape which looks more or less the same—might age or youthen based on what you're feeding it or how much light you're taking in. You might lose or gain mass, again depending on how much light you're taking in, what you're eating and so on. But you can recognize yourself: "Ah, this is the hub. This is the body-self." You, at the same time, lose interest to some degree in the body-self.

When you think that's all you are . . . You could think of models as a caricature of a type that focused very much on the physical, and would be extremely distraught if there was a disfigurement of face or body, or whatever that type of modeling career was based on. When you are aware that the body is holding something called an energetic field, a toroidal field of the heart, and that's what you're traveling through, you don't get so concerned if the body gets some gray hairs or gets short or fat over time, the compression of age and so on.

At the same time, you're going to have access to more youthening ideas through the galactic landscape. So we don't mean that aging will be the same either. But we don't see that you'll be so attached to what does the self look like when you have access to so many ways of perceiving and knowing.

At the same time, there is that sanity, sameness of the physical self to come back to. It's quite helpful. If you were to be one hour a butterfly, one hour a toad, and then a snake, and every time you came back to yourself you didn't know what you would look like, or how you hunt or fish, or how you drink water, it would be a little too much, even for the heart space. So there is the sameness of functionality, and yet nothing is at all the same.

You can use this hub and let it be, take care of it, but not be so attached to how that is when you realize how much wider the world is and yourself in it. And you begin to notice also through your travels, as your vision gets more fine-tuned, how you look different in different dimensions. That also helps with this loosening of the ego-self feeling: "Oh my goodness, if my body looks different or my hair looks different this day, people must be judging me." Or: "I feel a certain way about myself based on the apparatus of hairstyle and how the clothing fits today," and all of that.

Once you see how awkwardly you look in comparison in other dimensions, and perhaps strikingly beautiful in others—and all of that is you—you begin to lose this sense of "I need to hold on to and control what I look like all the time, because that's who I am or what I am to others."

The same could be said of your vantage points on Earth in life. For example, if you take a traditional human type, yourself 10 years ago, let's say, you had a certain way of walking on Earth, which means your vantage point is at eye level, more or less. Five to six feet, around there, is where you're viewing the world, as opposed to the bird aerial view or the angelic which is difficult to describe, but doesn't come through an eye point like that. Just by changing the perception, let's say, from human eye point to bird or dragon from above, you could imagine that what you notice is quite different.

Also, what you notice about yourself is quite different when you are looking from different vantage points. You begin to lose this fixed sense of judgment: "I am wonderful in these ways. I am horrible in these other ways." Because it becomes too much to categorize: "Well, I like these parts of my dragon self and these parts of my angelic. I don't know about this sort of more clinical, intellectual viewpoint of the Pleiadian."

If you're trying to sort it all here in the mind, there's too much conflict, because there's too much variety. Because you're now from the fifth-dimensional platform moving through the heart, you can take it in like that field of wildflowers. "Wow, there's part of me that sees things from a vantage point that's quite an overlook. And there's part of me that sees things straight in the eye. And there's part of me that's way distant and sees the whole planet at once." We'll speak about those vantage points yet to come. It's a richer experience, and you're not so homogenous.

But again, because you're traveling through the heart space, it doesn't feel incongruous. It feels instead that you loosen the hold of needing to control the world to be exactly how your old human self would want it—let's say, always too hot or too cold, or this color palette, or speak softly or speak loudly. Those kinds of things that have felt so important or crippling in a way. You judge yourself: "I never can speak up loud enough for people to hear me." That kind of thing. You just loosen and soften those judgments of yourself when you recognize how much more than that you are. Just so, so delightful to see how many aspects of self you have. Yet, because it's moving through the heart, that doesn't feel too lost.

The sense of third-dimensional, old human model was about control and contrast, right? "If I like it hot and it's cold outside, I feel that contrast, and I might try to control the temperature to be how I like it." When you have different selves that might like it, some hot, some cold, you can, in fact, lean into those parts of yourself that enjoy the atmosphere you're in. It's quite handy. The sense of discomfort or trying to control things, to be a certain way, is part of what falls away, along with the third-dimensional reality. Within your lifetime it will feel, begin to feel, a little bit like a myth: "I remember when . . ." You hear grandparents telling those stories of: "Remember when the town used to look like this? Or that tree was only this high? Now it's a canopy over our roof."

You are going to feel that way about third dimension, and almost think: "Could that have been true, that we were so linear, so boxed in and so much in a time/space continuum where things really took quite a lot of haste or measured effort, even if it was gentle effort over time. Where now, like rushing water that can get there so fast, or evaporate, or become a rain cloud and rain down—there's so many different creative ways to become or experience the world that you want.

Don't be frightened or alarmed if you start to loosen the sense of: "I need to control" or "I know what I like." Because when you can see from above, different viewpoints, you might like that you never did before. And that's all right, you're not losing yourself. Yourself is expanding. If any sense of alarm comes there, you just come into the sense of fluidity in the heart, whether that is focusing your physical energies there, or asking yourself questions like: "What do I want? What's alive for me right now?" Then you settle down because you become clear again: "What is my vantage point?" which is holistic.

You may start to have very different food cravings, even your sleep— as we have been talking about for some time—may change quite a lot. How much you sleep in one go, how much sleep you need to feel rested, even positions of sleep, like side or back and so on, may change. There's very little which isn't up in the air right now, in terms of the lived human experience.

If you can do one thing, it would be to drop that sense of judgment, of comparing: "What I know about myself is I need 7 ½ hours of sleep. I need coffee with breakfast. I need shade and not sun, this temperature, this color sweater . . ." It's not that you can't have all of those things, or at least once in a while. But don't be alarmed if you start to feel: "No, I really need four hours of sun and only four hours of sleep," or whatever it is. It may shift quite a lot back and forth and around.

Dropping this judgment that's based on anything that you could say, you could quantify or put into a list. "Here's the foods that are healthy for me. Here's the supplements that are healthy for me. Here's the diet regimen, the exercise and if I tarry from this, something's going to go wrong." If you're holding to that kind of control. It makes this transition time tricky, because you're putting judgment on the fact: "But I just want to sleep 10 hours tonight," or "I'm really craving soup." Whatever it is may be exactly what's needed for your dimensional leaning at that time.

Through experimentation, you can come to trust that a bit more. But we do want to say to the cerebral aspect of you, to the mind, please don't keep to that same list of: "I know if I do these things every day, I'll be healthy, or I'll be happy, I'll be sane." Because it's going to change. It's going to change quite a lot, and change again and change again.

Let's give a simple example. If you always felt: "I've checked with myself, if I get any less than 7 ½ hours of sleep, I feel terribly cranky, or I make mistakes at work." Then all of the sudden you're getting six or five hours because you're up for a few hours in the middle of the night, so the mind wants to say: "I'm tired, I'm cranky, I'm making mistakes." But pay attention. Is that really what's happening? Or do you feel fine during the day, but perhaps a little more relaxed than you used to? Or, you're actually not making mistakes? And how is that?

Well, what was happening in those hours when you were awake in the night? Perhaps it was a solar transmission or meditation of some kind, even though you didn't think that's what you were doing. So being honest with yourself and not comparing to an old list of yourself.

The sleep example is a good, relatable one. There will be many, many other ways this might show up for you. "I ate way too much. I'm probably going to be sick." Or: "I haven't been eating at all. What's wrong with me?" Yet, just pay attention. "What is my energy level? Is that, in fact, what my body craves right now for this particular transition, and is it all right? Does the body feel like it has the vibrancy and the aliveness that it wants?" Not forcing yourself: "No, no, no, no. I never eat a hot dog. I can't do that!" Or: "No, no, no, no, I don't eat broccoli." Maybe your dragon-self loves broccoli.

Flexibility is the most kind and helpful tool you can use for yourself, because the mind is not going to have this reference manual. "On Tuesdays, I should feed broccoli to my dragon-self, and on Wednesdays be out in the sun an extra hour." It's not going to be linear like that, right? Every Tuesday from now on will not look the same as the last.

That is the reality of being a hub with access to 12 dimensions. So the less that you can try for sameness or control, remembering that that is a very third-dimensional way of being. "There's a spectrum from hot to cold, and I'm going to control the temperature reading, or the blinds, the shades on the window, so that I have exactly that sameness of temperature, and then I'll feel all right." That's the old third dimensional way of living.

The beauty of the hub through fifth to 12 dimensions is you don't have to try to control along polarity spectrums anymore. "I always like it exactly this quiet, not too quiet, but not too noisy, and then I can focus." Maybe that's not true of yourself anymore. Being kind, it's not that you have to rush out and try, if you like quiet, put yourself in noisy environments and test it out. "Am I okay with noise now?"

It's more that it's going to come from a craving, not necessarily a food stomach craving, but a yearning for: "I want to be around more people right now. I really want to be in silence in the yard, or out in nature, on a trail." Honoring that, respecting as much as you can. Even, let's say, within a workplace which is fixed and you don't feel fluidity in, there's always times when you can add more towards those conversations at lunch and or more towards working on your own, when you want that more aliveness of people and conversation and more of the stillness and the witnessing. We don't want to say focus, but the silence will be necessary in some of these phases of transition.

Primarily today, we want you to understand yourself as you have known yourself—a body with a sensory experience, with a spiritual understanding, with a brain, with a heart, with a gut, all of that and many, many other ways of sensing the world—that is the hub, the place through which you travel. It's not you. It's not your fixed point, and that's it. Many of you are spiritually aware of that, but what happens now is the visceral awareness of life starts to match what you've known all along, which is: "I'm not limited to this one expression of soul, this body in this dimension." That's where the fun begins.

But some of you will feel here and there: "Wait, I'm losing my way. I can't make myself eat broccoli." Or: "I can't keep myself away from broccoli," whichever it is. "That means something's wrong."

If you can think of all of these—foods, medicines, types of light, types of interaction, or reading books or feeling quiet, not wanting many words in the mind—as all just being different calibrations, different expressions of the One. It doesn't matter which one you're in right now. It's going to feel a lot less like a need to control. And then you can let life surprise you.

Some of it will be through your own direction. "I want this," and then you receive it because you're craving it. "Somehow I'm craving being around people, craving the broccoli. I'm craving to quit coffee for an hour or a year." Following that inclination is the kindest way of navigating the fluidity of now.

These are all practical things, right? But the mind can freak out because its sense of identity and self is so built around the schedule and habits of daily life. That's where you can, with compassion, just hold this loosely in your awareness. "Okay, things might change and change again. It's alright if I start wanting to wear different colors of clothing or eat different things. It doesn't mean that I'm going through a midlife crisis, or a quarter-life crisis, or that necessarily even I'm changing who I am."

But you are expanding from this one dimension. Like a piece of paper —that's how thin you were in third dimension. Now you're like an origami—all these different shapes and different dimensional realities and different colors. The fabric of you is the same. That's why we say paper or origami—which is something like a crane or a flower bird that's made from folded paper. The substance of you, the Divinity, the life force of you, is the same as when you were in a thin dimension.

You were a gorgeous self in third dimension. And you have more angles of expression, more colors, more ways to refract light now. Don't be trying to iron out your origami to keep it straight and narrow!

If you were very quiet and shy, you might find suddenly you're the life of the party. Again, eating is patterns are going to change for many of you. And ways of perception. If you always had the narrow viewpoint, the details, you might suddenly be able to see the big picture.

Some of this might take [the form of] wonderful spiritual awakenings or the form of diverse expressions of looking into other dimensions. And it may look very wonderful or terrible, depending on how scared you get about new vistas, new viewpoints.

But it's also going to play out in the practical and the physical. That's why we're spending time on this today. If these habits of you change, just let them change. As long as you are not eating razor blades and candy bars all day long, and never moving from your chair. There are still some truths about health and the physical body. You know that. But maybe it's more sweets than you're accustomed to, and maybe it's more or less activity than you're accustomed to. Not holding that need to control what has worked in the past and continuing to try to iron out your origami shapes as they're forming. "No, no, no, no! I like it like this."

Allow that experimentation, almost like you're your teenage self. Not in the sense that we expect you'll be a very volatile with hormones or emotions, but in your teenage self, for most of you, you suddenly became interested in different things, and that was natural. That was right. Similarly, if you're suddenly interested in different types of books, different types of people, different colors, different foods, different sleep patterns, that's quite natural at this phase of your evolution.

It does become natural, feel normal, even to the mind over time. Once you've made lots of origami shapes out of yourself, the mind expects that of you, and no longer expects to be a flat piece of paper. But that takes a while, right? Meantime, don't be alarmed. "Wait, wait, I've got a sharp edge here, and I'm curling over here, and I'm a different color! And what's happening?!"

We're speaking metaphorically. Some of you will see visions and hear things that you don't know what to make sense of. But for most of you, where this plays out right now in your evolution is daily life—the habits and the cravings and whether or not you feel like being alone or with others. Don't worry. It's not just that you're in a mood or in a life change or life crisis. This is expansion of you.

14

FLUIDITY OF HEART

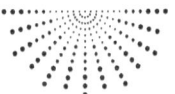

as the key that to access the other dimension it has to be through your heart and not through your head?

This is Rafael. Operationally, functionally, that means leaning in more and more to the heart space. Now the heart is where there is the efficient use of energetic force and will. It's not that we're talking about lean into "I am sad, I am glad" type of heart. But leaning into the current of energy, and you as the vortex or propeller of that. Shaping the world through your will. That's what we mean about leaning in through the heart.

The heart knows how to do that, because the heart knows how to create change. It's not so worried about the categories, because if it doesn't like what is, it just can shape and change it. Where the mind, if you think things are fixed in the third-dimensional way, it's very important. Let's say, if you're choosing a food to eat, to eat, the one that's not poison. Categories are very important, right? So it felt very life or death in third dimension to make the right choice. Because you're locked in there. Or you can't go back. You make a choice and you deal with the consequences.

The heart is more about leaning towards something. If it seems like sunny meadow and a good day: "I'll stay there longer." If it seems like a frigid morning: "I think I'll retreat; do something else." There's that fluidity of respond and react and shape with the environment, with other people, co-creation.

Whereas third dimension, you're seeing yourself as apart from, as distinct. This is me and my body. I have to choose certain things. I'm limited in my choices, and there are consequences to my choices and actions that cannot be undone. Now, there can be consequences multi-dimensionally, when you move energy or receive energy, but then you also know it's changeable for the most part. Some things like the death moment won't be, really. You can't go back and undo. But for the most part, things are so much more fluid. It's a very, very different way of perceiving and living in the world.

Do the angels have anything to say about judgment? Because even though I would prefer to be in my heart. The mind is still a little bit going to come up with judgments.

This is Raphael. Twelve-dimensional living, which will be an exploration, not something you get "right" right away, helps with this. Because the judgment that would come from your human self as you have known it--let's say the one that grew up with your family--and the judgment from your angelic self, the judgment from your dragon self, the judgment from your Pleadian self, are all going to be askew from one another. They're not going to really line up.

There might be some congruous parts and some incongruous parts to these different judgments. That's going to allow you, when you're in the heart space to see: "Oh, all these colors are woven into the same tapestry. That's where it's all all right. Because it's all part of the same large picture."

If you're trying to make the navy blue threads look like the red ones, it's never going to align that way, right? That's where the heartache can come with family, particularly. But when you notice how many different judgments or different ways of preference or perception are within you in your expanding self, it's going to be easier to let go of the fact that family members or people you don't know in politics live very different value-judgment lives. Just have a different way of seeing the world and acting in it.

Because you won't see it as a direct threat to yourself, it becomes less of an alarm. In family, the tension can sometimes be: We're all supposed to be alike, so which one of us is dominant, which gets to win? Are we all supposed to be like mother, or we all supposed to be like the bratty younger brother? Who is loudest in the family, sometimes seems like their values get to dominate. Yet some families or some people at a certain maturity of life, recognize: "Oh! It's really okay that we're all very different people. As long as we don't step on each other's toes of being who we are."

Twelve-dimensional expressions, explorations, help with that, because you start to learn how different you are from the different aspects of yourself, and how that is congruous through the heart space—you're just a wider picture of yourself, and that's alright. It becomes much easier to love, not just tolerate, people in your family or people you don't know in politics who have very, very different ways of being. Like different shapes of clouds, it doesn't occur to you to try to value a sky where the clouds are all the same shape. That happens sometimes. But on the days when the clouds are different shapes, it doesn't really occur to you that there's a problem with that. Someday you're going to look at your family, and it won't occur to you that there's any problem of how different they are.

I *s there anything like a practical, everyday thing that you can do to be more multi-dimensional?*

This is Rafael. Being open to surprise in the moment. One of the tensions in terms of third dimension versus multidimensionality is:

what really is in the present. Let's say I like to go for a dive every day at 7am or 4am, whenever it is, and yet, on this particular day, the conditions are not right, or they're right on a different time of day. In that moment, can I recognize that and act in that moment to harness something new where the energies are.

That can be difficult when you're trained that sameness and routine and organization are the right ways to get things done or to enjoy life. That is the biggest tension right now in terms of practical everyday life. So if yesterday, I planned to today have pasta for dinner, but today, a neighbor brought by a bunch of fresh zucchini from the yard, whatever it is, can I adjust and make that instead. Being open to the positive surprises of life and not saying, "Oh, that's a great idea for another time. I'll set that aside." But "Oh, well, this is ripe and fresh. Let's eat this right now."

Changing the "plan." That's the most practical way of meeting interdimensionality. Now, it doesn't seem like that. That skill of being in the moment: "What is present right now?" serves you when you are dealing with multiple currents of energy. Because very rarely, our multidimensional energy is going to fit increments—like time increments or money deposit increments or measured growth, like company growth that could be measured and planned. The more that you can, let's say, receive the positive surprises, that is best. That's the most practical way to meet these energies.

Could the angels give any idea of the component of humanity who is ascending? In terms of what they outlined on Friday night, is that component 50% close to what they were describing? Are they 10%? Is it fair to ask something to give us an idea of where on that trajectory the ascending group are?

This is Raphael. The way we see it, humanity is like at the edge of an open meadow or open field. So it's open. It's not that special codes are needed, or bridges or anything like that, or ascension codes, or the right moment, or the right astrological forecast. But many people, let's say, coming towards the meadow from buildings, corridors and structure, will look out and say: "It doesn't look safe. I don't have the protection of my box here. I'm going to retreat back, see what other people do first, or just face the other direction."

The choice point is there. It's open. In terms of how many people are exploring, walking around the meadow and then maybe going back, because it feels: "I'd like to rest in a structure, because I recognize that." Maybe 10%, more or less, are already in the exploration phase.

Again, it's open to everyone. We see very few so far who feel, in terms of habitat, that the open plane of exploration is where they live. It's more explore and then go back home to the structure, right? Explore and then go back home. That will shift. Where structure is dissolved and not returned to, very few are in that state of being yet.

*I*s the angels' hope that this pulse of humanity that's on the Earth at the moment, that maybe 30% of humanity would ascend? Or is that silly to even think about numbers?

This is Rafael. It's about right. From our vantage point, that's probable. We're talking about this round. In other words, people alive on Earth right now, in this lifetime.

Now, almost 100% of those coming in right now and in the next generation, are already 12-dimensional. So in terms of the sea change of humankind, that's a given. In terms of people who are "left behind," so to speak, or not yet there, not everyone chooses to do that this go around. But they'll have other chances to do that. And we don't see them as stuck or that they can't.

To us, because it's open and because the sea change has happened for humankind, we don't see it as so important how many choose it in this life. Because the multitude or the masses, enough people have jumped over that it now is viable and alive as an open field for humankind. That's what the angelic was seeking—the openness, the freedom to choose.

15

HOW DO I CHOOSE OR KNOW WHAT DIMENSION I AM IN?

This is Angel Raphael. We speak about the dimensions as if there are 12. And you also know now about your galactic lineage strains of new DNA, of which there are 12. *The question arises, are those interlinked?* Does the DNA strand related to dragon or the DNA strand related to angelic correspond to a particular dimensional field? The answer is yes. The 12 that we will be playing with you to explore that are now locked in, in a beautiful way through you as the hub (in through the navel out through the heart and so on). They do correspond with dimensional fields. Which means, essentially, you are the avatar of yourself in all of these 12 dimensions.

If you are plucking the string or activating your dragon galactic energetics, and then you are asking to travel into that dimensional field, you have the best set of perceptual skills to move around easily. Now, can you just go as yourself, which is a conglomerate, or you're not quite sure yet? Yes, you can. We've done that in the past—interdimensional travel, just as you innocently exploring.*

---

* English-language course on interdimensional travel available online at www.adriaestribou.love/shop

However, you're going to find the best success, the best resonance and Interplay when you use the corresponding aspect of yourself. We also want to note that in terms of dimensional fields, there are many more than 12, and it does get somewhat fractal. You are not limited to the 12 galactic strands, to those dimensional fields. However, those are the ones that you have easiest access to, and so those are the ones that we start with, because that's plenty to be getting on with. Once you've mastered the 12, or perhaps, if instinctually, you're invited or drawn somewhere else, and it doesn't match with the 12, we just want to mention it's all right, you're not making things up, most likely. It's just that there are more than 12. However, in this book we're just going to focus on the 12, continuing until all of those activations are explored.

The question also arises, do we all have the same 12? And the answer is yes. In terms of New Earth Human, 12-dimensional human, there are the same 12 dimensions and the same 12 galactic lines.

You still are quite unique as an aspect of soul, as an individual. When you're talking about, let's say, the etymology of a grasshopper—well, they all have the same kind of organ types and legs or wings or spectrum of colors and so on. Similarly, the New Human, this 12-dimensional human, is the same. There's not, let's say, between you and your sister or brother six in common, but you have a different six for the other to make up 12 different. You had dragon and your friend or sister has fairy kingdom there. No, they're all the same 12. What you do with those abilities, those skills, is very unique. That's where your soul expression comes into play.

As we'd said, this is a choice point, one among many, to activate these new galactic lines of DNA. For those who choose not to activate that in this lifetime, it's like a dormancy. You've seen that in your medical sphere with latent dis-ease. Sometimes there are things that are there that are just never triggered in the lifetime. Similarly, there can be things that are there on the positive and that are just never triggered in the physical self.

Those who are choosing not to move into these 12-dimensional ways of being as the New Human still look the same as you on the outside, but they're not going to be able to relate to being able to fly or perceive things through dragon eye and so on. Not because they are shut off, shut down, blocked from, or judged as wanting in any way, but because their soul is choosing: "Yeah, for right now, I'd rather stay in three-dimensional, linear existence. I'd like to be able to measure things out. I'd like to be able to have a plan. I enjoy polarity in that spectrum of push/pull, because I know where I stand." There's reasons for that as a soul.

Now, when you're moving into the more fluid 12 dimensions, you're not all of the 12 all at once. You're generally leaning into one or three at a time. Let's say fourth/fifth dimension is your resting place. You might be drawing on Pleiadian, angelic and one other galactic strand in your resting place while you're writing a book or talking to a friend. Some sense of intuitive knowing is coming forward. You see things in a different way, maybe not through the physical eye, but you're able to take a broader view. Maybe when you're thinking about your friend's life, you think: "Oh, I have this wider perspective, or non-judgmental view—seems to match more with angelic viewpoint." You're activating that in yourself.

We don't see from angelic perspective, that any of the 12 are higher or best in you. However, you will have favorites, and that will likely change as you grow up, move on. You might be very, very enamored with your dragon-self for a while and get very close, akin to how that works and how that influences you. Then you might shelve that for a little while, because there's someone else you're meeting or something you're growing into that requires more of a Pleiadian intellect or Arcturian, and so on.

One of the ways you're going to be able to map where to go next, or how to tell where you are, is by linking that with your growing understanding of what is this dimensional galactic being strand. We'll keep picking on dragon here, playing with dragon a bit. When we say dragon galactic DNA, we don't really mean that there's one dragon that you are. We use the word avatar. It's not that you are a purple dragon with green eyes and four wings or something like this, a certain length of tail, and that's who you are as your dragon-self.

It is more that within that purity of galactic strand of dragon—there may be earth dragon, water dragon, air dragon, sensibilities—all of the spectrum of dragon is available. The dragons, like humans (old humans), had similarities: the way they view things, the way they fly . . . You come to recognize: "Oh, when I smell things in a certain way, or when I treasure/value things in a certain way, when I become protective in a certain way that doesn't have fear with it—is more of a masculine protective energy that is love-based—I think I track that with my dragon-self, so I might be more in the dimension of dragons."

Let's say, for your human physical self you wanted to resource what dragons know about health, so you might get more into color therapy or mineralogy, or crystal healing. Crystals overlap with other dimensions as well. You could bring consciously into dragon dimension. If you were healing someone else, the fact that you are resonating in that dimension will draw them in a bit, or resonate the frequency of that in them while you're working together. You can help to awaken others' gifts or dimensional lines by resonating strongly there.

Whether or not you use those words is not important. It could freak some people out to say: "Oh, great. I'm going to just go dip into the dragon dimension here to bring in some color therapy for you." They might leave the building very quickly. But if you just say: "Oh, I'm seeing some green light. Let's put that into your jaw here, and just feel that." You can use words that can resonate more widely, but this is more for you to know as you understand what the dimensions are.

We are not in the course of this work going to give the dimensions numbers with you. We think it's more instructive to say dragon or angel or Pleiadian dimension, because that will bring up a whole bunch of different markers for you. More so than trying to memorize what is three, what is seven, what is 13. Also because the human mind likes to think the 12th dimension is higher, or first dimension is higher, and have them as a spectrum that's a linear that you move through one then the next and then the next, so that you have to travel through seventh and eighth to get to ninth. That's incorrect. Again, you are the hub. You can access any of them direct from you. It's not a hierarchy. The number one or the number 12 is not the highest one. They're just distinctly different.

The question arises: is third dimension, then, one of these 12 galactic strands? It is not. We're working with higher conscious energies now. Which is another reason why we're not numbering them. It doesn't quite make sense. Third dimension is the platform, or the base that you used to live in. Fourth/fifth is what you live in now. Beyond that, still, are these 12 dimensions that are galactic dimensions.

Some beings are interdimensional and can walk through different dimensions, as can the New Human. When you are in a realm that has giants in it, you might also see fairies or unicorns. You'll learn which are the primary beings in that dimension, or, let's say, the set. Sometimes in Inner Earth you might find trolls, munchkins—they've been called different things in different places of the world. You might find a set of two or three types of beings together.

That's how you can make your map—partly how it changes you, how you feel different, and partly, if you're visual, what you're seeing when you're there. In this example, giant is one of the 12 galactic strands of DNA. Many fairy tale stories about giants here, let's say, in this dimension. They are friendly. Nothing you have to worry about here. Giants do not live on their own. You'll see other beings in that dimension.

EXPLORATION: GIANT DIMENSION

Adria: For the following exploration, I suggest reading the text below first. Then ask (out loud or silently) for Angels Raphael and Ariel to be with you as you explore. You may want to sit quietly after that with your eyes closed or open and witness what you perceive.

This is Angel Raphael. Let's go there now together, because we have not explored giants yet. Just through your own intent, let's ask to perceive a friendly dimension of giants. And to be informed about what that means in your own human new DNA structure, to have giant energies.

One thing we will point out as you're gently moving into this yourself —a little storytime here—there is a fairy tale legend about seven league boots. This is about giants. In other words, the ability to jump continents. You can do that as a giant, as your giant-self.

In addition to flight, which dragon and angelic carry—physical flight —giants can take large leaps, you can also move that way as your giant-self, particularly in the dimension of giants. Remember that these dimensions are overlapping on what you call Earth.

Just asking to experience a little what it is like to be in the giant dimension, and what that informs in your own consciousness.

Just perceiving, witnessing whatever it might be. Again, you're not necessarily going to have the whole picture, the whole sound or the whole smell all at once. But one of these might tug at you a little bit. Just noticing what you perceive, either in you or in the external environment.

Giants, from angelic historic viewpoint, came as galactic beings to Earth before humankind. They make up one of the 12 strands of your new human DNA.

Very gently, bringing yourself back to this platform of fourth/fifth dimension.

I felt almost holographic. I found that very interesting. I would have thought I would have had more mass as a giant, but I felt extremely light, and like all my cells were just vibrating. I was very concerned about my feet and trampling people when I was going from continent to continent. But it was very light.

This is Rafael. As a wider point here, let's consider the holographic nature of the universe versus density and light. At some times you may, each of you, become aware of what appears to be refracted light, or somehow an unreal sense of manipulation of sound and light to create a fake environment. The worlds, each of the dimensions, are essentially created like this.

Within that, there can be this felt sense of lightness or density. Both are accurate. It's no less "real" to be in the holographic state than in the one where you feel very grounded, rooted and bouncy, jubilant, or heavy in the physical sense—as a general comment. Giant is not, let's say, more holographic than is dragon or your old human way of viewing. When you are in a certain lightness of being, you might perceive the holographic nature of the universe more readily.

The angels mentioned that the giants came before humans, if I understood that correctly. And there's also galactic connection. What is the galactic connection and why would the giants have come to Earth?

This is Angel Raphael. Well, to simplify, any being, essentially, on Earth—conscious, sentient being—is off planet. Earth didn't start out full with peoples of different kinds, and so it did require some sort of transport. Not everyone uses a spaceship, but some sort of transport to arrive here.

Giants were among the first species to explore Earth. They have remained contiguous. In a historic sense, there have always been giants on Earth. However, they are not often enfolded in third dimension. It's not impossible, but it's rare to see them there.

Are yetis and giants the same thing?

Essentially, yes. This is Angel Raphael. They share a dimension, and they are hybrids or leanings of one another, so they're related. You can distinguish giant from yeti, but it's not important to do so in terms of this exercise. The way we were talking about dragons that are earth or air based, there's a distinction between giant and yeti, but they are the same type of galactic being—humanoid, larger than typical third-dimensional human. They do have distinguishing characteristics, but if you have a leaning towards one or the other it's all right. If you feel more curious or safer exploring one over the other using this word yeti or giant, you could interchange them.

Does that include sasquatch or in Australia, there's a different name, yowie?

Absolutely, this is Ralphael. Part of this is similar to how tribes of humankind, third-dimensional humans, have called themselves by different tribal names, and have to some extent adapted to their environment. We're talking about not huge evolutionary changes, but skin pigments or size of ears or something depending on jungle or desert landscape, eye color and so on to adapt to the quality of light. We're talking about the third-dimensional humans over time.

Similarly, sasquatch, yes, is more of a regional name for the same thing. Of course, there can be differences socially, and in terms of pigments or other visual cues, some differences, but those are the same type of being.

. . .

Can I ask if giants have a particular role in New Earth?

This is Rafael. Simplicity of heart is one of giant's gifts. A giant, if it were to see a bird out of a nest or a small child on its own, the inclination would be to pick up and hold in the hands and carry it somewhere safe. Not necessarily to have the curiosity of intellect: "What type of species is this? Why did it fall?" and all of that. It is the simple instinct of the heart to mend, to protect, to clothe, to feed, those kinds of things.

Also, there is a quietness. Third-dimensional humans have to spend so much time in meditation to quiet down the mind. Giants come with a quietness of mind, which is not the same as being stupid, or dumb. They are not chatty like that in the mind, typically speaking. If you encounter a giant and sit with them, they may not have very many words, but you're going to feel that friendship is very paramount. And the simplicity of heart. Heart wants to outreach and help in a tender way. Those are some of the characteristics, in addition to speed of travel, as we've mentioned.

On the spectrum of giants some, like yeti, are highly interdimensional, so you see them everywhere, across all 12 dimensions. Some of the giants have rooted themselves a little more in time and place, and don't like to travel so much.

I went to school in Nevada, and that's when I first heard about this discovery that was made, I think in the early 1900s, of this cave out in the middle of the desert. There's a bunch of petroglyphs, I think that have giants in them, and a bunch of artifacts. And this was from like 10,000 years ago or something, when there was actually an inland sea. They found canoes and stuff like that. In the cave was this giant shoe, or slipper-type thing. I always wondered if that was really a shoe for a giant, or maybe it was like made by humans to honor giants, or something like that?

This is Raphael. If you pay attention, there are different archeological finds around the world that are consistent with the idea—giant behavior, and size of head, and so on. Sometimes they're just unexplained mysteries. Or people wonder, was that an anomaly? From an angelic perspective, the giants have been here all along, and still are here. They are physical beings, but again, not often these days in third dimension.

Is it true that the giants moved the pillars that were used to build Stonehenge?

The short answer is yes. This was Raphael. Other beings were involved in the design in terms of the meaning, astrologically, you might say, or alignment with the star beings and interplanetary travel. There was a design there, archeological design, and other species were involved. Giants did help with the moving. Each dimension doesn't just have one type of being. And again, some beings, giants among them, can move interdimensionally.

We can take an aside here for a moment. Some religions or folk traditions or things that are passed on through word of mouth, down the ancestral lines in humankind it's hard to make sense of. Let's say it's been interpreted or misinterpreted through the years. Someone saw a giant, and it becomes something else as it's passed down through generations, or the understanding of what a giant was doing there—to help with the building Stonehenge or something—that could certainly be interpreted many different ways, and in a future religious context, perhaps they would cast a negative light on such a thing, even though it was quite neutral or positive at the time.

This is where you get to be innocent with your exploration, and keep some of these ideas. "Well, this might be true. I read this somewhere." It might match closely to what you had heard or read, and might be very different in your own exploration of these different dimensions. Certainly, from angelic standpoint, the giant dimension as it is accessible to you now and is part of your pure galactic DNA, is quite friendly, is quite beneficent. It is not of the dark or ill intent.

∾

EXPLORATION: GIANT FRIENDSHIP

Adria: For the following exploration, as with the exploration above, I suggest reading the text below first. Then ask (out loud or silently) for Angels Raphael and Ariel to be with you as you explore. You may want to sit quietly after that with your eyes closed or open and witness what you perceive.

This is Raphael. Let's do one more exercise with the giants. If you want to, keep yourself in fourth/fifth, and because giants, yeti, sasquatch are interdimensional beings, you could ask if there are any in your area that are friendly to you and compatible with what you're learning and growing into. If there's any that would like to visit you now, to make themselves known in some gentle way. You can have your eyes open or closed for this. You are essentially staying in your comfort-zone dimension (fourth/fifth) and inviting a giant or yeti to visit with you, to cross dimensions to be seen or heard or felt or known as a friend.

Just gently, if you met a friend, you could invite them to visit more often.

They might take you with them to their dimension on another adventure day. That's one way to travel interdimensionally is to ride the coattails, so to speak, of giants passing through. (Not literal coattails).

∾

Should we ask these beings how they can help us? Or should we suggest to them what it is we feel we need?

This is Raphael. Giants are social creatures, so for them it will be more about friendship first. In other words, you could express: "I'd like to be your friend. Would you like to be my friend?"

Some other beings, like Pleiadian for example, might have more of a direct connection like that, to be able to ask: "What is our purpose in meeting here? Should I be serving the Pleiadian somehow? Or do you have knowledge that could help me serve humankind?"

This will depend on the type of being. It's nice to meet beings where they are, same as when you meet new human friends. We would say, in general, it's always nice to share your intent. Whether that is first just emanating a bit of love out of your heart space, or a smile energetically with your heart or with your face to just say: "Wow, welcome. It's so fun!" Or: "It's an honor to meet you." You can just start that simply. Just to share the positivity there, and to feel if it's reciprocal.

Again, the interchanges relating you into are quite friendly ones, so we don't anticipate anything other than that. And it's nice for you to feel that. More important than getting right to the finer spiritual grains of thought here, there is this whole aspect of humankind moving into a more collaborative, cooperative nature. And part of that is these other beings. When you're collaborating or cooperating, it's also as simple as friendship or getting to know this being exists. And that can be enough.

When humans meet other humans, we have niceties at the start of conversations. We're not like: "Hi, could you give me the solution to pollution?" But I noticed that when you deal with intergalactic beings, there's no niceties. It's like, bang straight in. Is that the same with all the other dimensions? Do we act like with other humans? Or do we mirror what they're doing, which feels a bit rude?

This is Raphael. It's going to depend on you, and it's going to depend on the type of being. You're right. Humans tend to be very focused on:

"Let's get right to what's important here." Not human to human, necessarily. But when you're looking at getting wisdom from Ascended Masters or galactic beings, you really often do skip that part. "Who are you? And I'm so glad you're here!" But just: "Hey, can you tell me how my soul can evolve?"

Yes, that's a bit of a human trait. Although, interestingly, you don't exhibit that to one another. In fact, you rarely get to that kind of kernel of truth in a social sense with other humans.

We would suggest it's a good practice to start again with this emanating some love from the heart space or sense of welcome, so they know what you're about. And then you can proceed from there: "So glad you're here. Are you just here visiting and curious about me? Or was there a reason? Did you have some message today?" You could feel into it that way. It will be a mix of both.

16
WHY NOW? THE 12 DIMENSIONS FOR HUMAN EXPRESSION

This is Angel Raphael. We want to give a bit of a historic take on what's going on right now. By right now we mean this year, more or less, in human expression, but also the turning point from what was—let's say, we're beginning to call the old human, or Old Earth Human, which is the one you grew up in, and the new consciousness expressed through new humanity, which is still going to look the same, more or less, from the outside.

This is the new type of human expression we've been speaking about. The 12 dimensions of galactic DNA expressed through each human form—those who sign up to be part of the new human expression. By sign up, we mean consciously, either before they came into this life or now—at any point from now forward—their consciousness says: "Hmm, yeah, I'd like that. I'd like to open up to my new gifts and new ways of perceiving."

It is very much a new type of evolutionary human—on a cellular level, on a functional level. And perception is quite important here, because when you're talking about synthesis of knowledge, different vantage points on perception are very instrumental.

This has been called the "learning planet," Earth, and the ways of learning in third dimension had a lot to do about expression of duality. And then there was the non-dual—some spiritual folks talking about the non-dual, which is what is beyond duality (hot/cold, light/dark, and so on). We have said that the time of learning is more or less complete with the conclusion of the old type of human.

What else is Earth about now? As you move into the realm of these 12 different ways of perceiving, it has a lot more to do with synthesis of knowledge. In other words, what is the lived expression, or a lived experiment of knowledge. As opposed to learning—what the soul came here to learn, and then exit through something called death, and move on to other expressions of being or learning.

Now, when you come into the synthesis of what we know collectively, galactically, now as the 12-dimensional human, the synthesis of knowledge means holding all of these vantage points and flowing through which ones feel best at any hour, at any given time, for the pure enjoyment of the synthesis of knowing.

Some have called this embodiment—embodiment of light, embodiment of knowledge. That is also correct. Today we'll speak in terms of synthesis, but it is the same. When you're talking about the lived expression of synthesis, you can substitute the word "embodiment" for "synthesis," if you like.

What does it mean to be the vantage point of synthesis? Instead of in duality—perhaps on the spectrum of light and dark, good and ill-will, you picked somewhere in the middle, or "I'm fighting for light." Then that's your vantage point. Those who are less light than you are perhaps "not as bright" might be your vantage point. Or: "they are dark." That's a judgment or a perception from a particular vantage point.

Now, when you are the synthesis of 12 different galactic ways of seeing—angelic, dragon, Pleiadian, Lyran and so on—what is that like? How do you have so many vantage points at once? Well, as we have said, you won't necessarily be active in 12 at any given hour—maybe two or three or one. And not the same ones, although you'll have favorites as you come to explore and define yourself in the new ways of being.

Synthesis allows for the different vantage points without feeling conflict or the need to define one in contrast to the other. If you were look through a prism, for example, a crystal with many facets, and hold it up to the light, you can see many things at once: the color of the crystal, the opacity, how the light shines through, where the different cuts are made, maybe one has a reflective surface . . . But you don't see those as being in conflict with one another, those different ways of viewing the same object. You are synthesizing the knowledge.

You're doing quite a lot when you just look at one semi-opaque crystalline structure held up to the light. You are viewing many different things at once, and yet you don't feel in conflict about that.

Similarly, when you're living the synthesis of knowledge of these galactic beings now active within you, there's not a conflict. Because you're not trying to define this vantage point is correct, or this vantage point means that someone else in my life story is incorrect.

Let's stay with the example of holding a semi-opaque crystal up to the light. You're just noticing: "Ah. Dragon sees in this the mineralogy and what it can sing into life. Angel sees, how does this help or guide my human friend (the human I am assigned with here)? Pleiadian sees how that same mineral has caused war in the past." Pleiadians are great historians. "Lyran remembers those crystals at the bottom of a lake in a musical expression of life (past-life memory there that is in the collective Lyran experience)."

Nowhere in yourself are you fighting for which of these vantage points is correct. For the most part, they will not have a direct conflict. They're not going to give you contradictory or misinformation. It is a lot to take in at once. But your mind knows how to process that much at once. That's why the mind is on your side, and not a hindrance in the spiritual evolution here.

Because the mind can notice that just in the simple act of holding a semi-opaque crystal up to the light, so much is going on. The mind can do that much computational analysis at the same hour and not feel in conflict about it. In this example, it is not "my crystal is better than yours." It is just observation.

There is a lot more of a sense of witnessing life. Not clinically. You can still enjoy it very much. You can love the color as it hits the light. But it's not about anything in a judgmental sense. It's not about a struggle and who's doing best in the struggle. It's not about a polarity. In which end of the polarity do I find myself: rich or poor? Those kind of dualistic natures of viewing the world don't really come into it.

MANIFESTING IN THE WRONG DIMENSION

You're in an evolution. Ten years ago, you were the old human. You had certain wishes that were on that polarity spectrum—for example, poverty and wealth, sickness and health. As you evolve into a way that is more of synthesis of knowledge and multidimensional perception, it's why when you wish for the things that were on those old duality planes—for example, money--sometimes doesn't come through as clearly as when you wish for something that's more multidimensional or more visionary. Or something that comes from curiosity, or interplay with the natural world, or evolution of consciousness.

Some of those answers and experiences and expression and perceptions can come through much more readily, easily than those things you used to wish for on a duality plane. Pay attention to that. Sometimes when wishes aren't coming through, and 20 other wishes are, the one you feel a bit stuck on, maybe think of: "If I was a dragon, how would I wish for this?" Or: "If I was an angel, how could I phrase this?" So that you can get what you want, but move it multidimensionally.

We use the example of a house, since this is something that many people admire. "I'd like to have a house." Or: "I like that I have a house." In the three-dimensional polarity view, that was where on the spectrum of how much money or how much work or how much time it was going to take to get a house.

Now, when you look at the multidimensional view of the house, it might be more now: What is the purpose of the house? Is it in a place on the land that's resonant with others, or apart from anyone else? Is it on a lay line that's important to me? Is it in a conscious community? Is it owned, or is that not important? What are the new measures of what used to be sense of security? What are the new parameters? Is it that it allows multidimensional beings to visit without disturbing neighbors? Is it that it allows yourself to grow in these expressions of multidimensional living? Is it that it is near a portal of some kind so that you can have greater interaction with some of these beings from dimensions other than fourth or fifth?

In both examples, you get to have a house. But in the first example it meant something about security. It meant something about money. It meant something about work and what was earned. Those are all polarities or valuations that made sense in third dimension.

It's not so simple when you come into the 12 dimensions of you. You can still have the same thing that you desire—in this case, a house—but the more that you explore, are curious about the why—What would that mean in a multidimensional sense?—the easier it is for the universe to support that. Because the you and the universe that you're reflecting are no longer resonating in that linear third-dimensional plane.

You're trying to create or manifest there; you are not there. Why would you manifest something that is in a dimension you are not in?

None of the 12-dimensional aspects of yourself that are coming in are very third-dimensional. Reptilian is a little bit, but Reptilians are also multidimensional. Strictly speaking, none of the 12 dimensions of you are third-dimensional. So when you're trying to create in third dimension, that's the problem. You're not, in fact, there. It's like living in Spain and trying to create a house in Paris. You have to do it by proxy. But then, if you're in Spain, why do you want a house in Paris?

We don't have judgment against third dimension, but when you've chosen to move into the 12-dimensional aspect of yourself to evolve in this way, it is no longer relevant for your expression. Again, you can still have money. You can still have a house. But if it's not coming through—whatever you're wishing for—very easily, it's likely that you're trying to manifest in a dimension you are not in. That's not impossible. But again, you need a proxy. And then again, you're not there. So why do you need something in a dimension you're not in?

Let's clarify here. Your body is still present, physical, able to live in a house. That is true for the multidimensional you, as well as it used to be in the third-dimensional aspect of yourself. You're still a physical being. We're not talking about becoming the ethers or consciousness that's abstract. All of this is quite concrete. It just has different rules of being. You still are a soul in a body. The body has changed. The soul has not necessarily. Souls can evolve, but that's not what we're talking about here. We're talking about the rules of the universe that you live and play in.

WHY 12 DIMENSIONS?

To go back to our theme today, our question: why would humanity choose to move from a two-dimensional sort of aspect, two strand DNA, to 12 galactic DNA activation? Consciousness gets bored. The way some ages of you, you outgrew what you were interested in then. It did not mean that what you loved as a six-year-old was in any way bad, or not highly evolved. But consciousness gets bored. It wants to learn something new, to express something new.

Most painters don't paint the same painting, 12 a day, on and on for the rest of their lives. Each time it's a little different. Or a lot different. Or they grow tired of painting, and want to be at the potter's wheel. The simple answer is: consciousness is evolving into more complex modes of reality.

WHY NOT HOW

It is not of service, we would suggest, to think of humanity as a petri dish experiment. In other words, sometimes when people learn about galactic influences in the DNA and the fact that humans are, by and large, engineered, there is this sense of fear and dread and ache. "What do you mean? I thought I was a biological being and natural. Was I manipulated? Am I created by something other than God?"

The way we view things, angelic, all of this is an expression of consciousness. And so when you have consciousness getting more and more fractal or more and more interplay with itself, you have now instead of just one race creating more and more babies, you have these 12 races creating something new. It's that simple.

Now the biomechanics of it are not so important here for this particular transmission, for your knowledge at this time. Those of you who are interested can delve into that. It's open knowledge, more or less. But it's not very important or useful, we would say, to consider the science of how this happened. Much more interesting is _why_ would consciousness evolve from a more limited being to a more complex one?

Simply said, it is the evolution of your consciousness—of _your_ consciousness reaching out to itself and playing more and more complex harmonies and rhythms on the notes of existence. The simple harmonies and rhythms were also extraordinary.

The 12-dimensional human is not better than two-dimensional human. But it is more evolved. It is more complex. And it has different rules of being. From an angelic perspective, both are loved.

ANGELS WITHIN AND ALONGSIDE

Now we will speak for a moment about angels relative to the two-dimensional and 12-dimensional human. Angels, as we have said, are very tied with humankind. With the birth of each human child, there are angels who come along with that life, through the whole life expression. Now in the 12-dimensional human, angel is one of the strands that are active within you.

For a little while, you will also have angels outside of yourself, because we have no need to abandon, so to speak, abandon humankind. However, we may be de-emphasized here. That's up to you, all of you.

We are one of 12 influences now. And we are very much within you, as well as outside of yourself. So for a little while, you have both. You have the angelic activated within you, and physical beings of light called angels who are around you in your soul expression. The same angels, in most cases, as were with you 10 years ago when you were the two-dimensional human. Those are personal angels. Your guides come with you through this massive transition. Perhaps you know them more intimately now. Perhaps you need them more or less in different phases of your evolution.

But this will change. Must change, right? If angels are now within you as part of your expression, maybe some generations down the road, only through conscious intent, will that change. Not because anything's wrong. But maybe you don't need to have three personal angels with you, if you are very in tune with the angelic strand within you. For now, angels are still very much with you. We're talking about the evolution of humankind over generations.

$\sim$

ENERGY EXERCISE: SYNTHESIS

English-language audio of this meditation is available available free online with the link at the end of the book.

As you read the following, please know that the invitation from the angels to work with your energies as they describe below is for you. (If you want them to!) Pause as often as you like while reading to breath and feel any energies, thoughts, or emotions that are inspired by Angel Ariel's words.

This is Angel Ariel. Let's do an exercise here, because ultimately this is not a mental exercise. The 12-dimensional human is not a mental exercise. It is one of synthesis. We are going to exercise your synthesis muscles.

If you'd like to sit in a chair or a lie or stand leaning on something so that you can let your attention rest inward. Good not to attempt to drive and so on while doing this kind of angelic exercise. Again, we want to feel the harmony within you. Although you're not perhaps aware yet of what are all of the 12 strands, there is a synthesis, a harmony to what is coming active in you. It's like a harp that's always in tune. We play a few notes, or 12 notes or 24 notes. It sounds lovely. You are a very forgiving instrument; the songs that you play quite lovely.

We're just working with your energies a little bit here to help with your direct expression, experience of the synthesis of you. You're not being pulled in different directions and being asked to choose. In the past, if you had two impulses—light and dark—they were on a spectrum of polarity, and you were being asked to choose one over the other. Now, if you have two impulses, let's say angel and dragon, they're not at war with one another. They're just different viewpoints. And they both belong with you, so there's a synthesis of how they come together through your life expression.

We want to empower you to feel that and know that through the energetic fabric of yourself; you are a synthesis of the knowing that occurs from these 12 galactic streams of activation.

"I am a synthesis" is a phrase, an aphorism, here you might want to post up on your wall to remind you, if you feel a little bit pulled in different directions or scattered, spaced out. Just remind yourself: "I am a synthesis."

"I am," which is one of the beautiful notes of expression, the vibration "I am" now has these 12 strands within it. It's more nuanced. It's more rich. This "I am" as it plays on the notes of you has so much more depth to it now. And it is not in struggle. These vantage points are not in struggle within you or between you and others in the human expression. Because now is a time of synthesis, not a time of battle, or contrast, or polarity.

When knowledge is synthesized, you feel whole. You feel digested. The meal is well digested.

There is no conflict within you from the different vantage points. They bring a richness and a depth to your expression, that's all.

You as a human are, in fact, more well-rounded now, just not in ways that you used to imagine. All of this is occurring inside your being. You don't have to look outside yourself so much for guidance, support and the synthesis of what you know.

Your "I am" now carries all of these many notes in it.

Resting for a moment in this "I am" and feeling the reverberation of the richness, the density field of so many interacting cosmos inside you—galactic beings from across the universe and from right here, synthesized in how you live this "I am." You are the culmination of generations of galactic being.

"I am."

All these vantage points sing In harmony: "I am."

Coming gently into the outer expression of your "I Am," which might mean wiggling your toes or looking about the room.

~

This is Raphael. As you are coming back into more outward expression of your consciousness, we will answer this question.

This is Adria. Someone had written: "Is there so much chaos in the world because consciousness is just bored?" It's a marvelous question.

This is Raphael. Chaos and order could be viewed from third-dimensional perspective, where order, for the most part, was what was valued by you. Another way of viewing this is that third dimension had a certain set of rules and parameters, and now when you come into multidimensional life, you are synthesizing rules and parameters from 12 different dimensions. And none of those 12 are the ones that you grew up in. That's a lot to synthesize.

When you're speaking about global circumstance or planetary awareness, and there appears to be chaos, understand that consciousness is being lived out through these different touchpoints called humans. Each of these different touchpoints might have very different vantage points and success measures. Many humans on the planet now are still in third-dimensional consciousness, striving still for health and wealth and light or dark or things along those polarities. And they're not always wishing for the same thing. Because that is on the polarity spectrum, there can be this push/pull, this belief that "either I get it or you get it," the battle cry. That is part of the chaos here.

But there is a disruptive nature of breaking down the barriers to multidimensionality, and essentially that is more of what you feel is chaos right now. There's a letting go of order and structure—the world as you have known it. And coming into synthesis and harmony. It's not that it will be chaotic in a misinformation sense, in a sense that: "I'll never know what's coming. One day the sky will be purple; the next day it will be green."

We want you to know how much you can change the world, so that might look like chaos. "Wait a minute, everyone can just decide on their own?!?" Yes, they can.

But once you come to playfully understand your role in the universe and your abilities in it, it doesn't feel like chaos anymore. It feels like multi dimensionality. But you are not "in control" of the whole universe. There are other touchpoints, other humans, also expanding in consciousness or staying in dense fields, wanting things, pushing for things, efforting for things, being fluid with the energies . . . A little bit like this painting behind here on the wall, the marbling or interplay of energies that could look like chaos, or if you look at it on any edge, it is the interaction of one color with another. So it depends on your vantage point.

*I*s it the pattern for each galactic civilization that they move to 12 strands of DNA in a similar way to the Earth? In effect, inheriting perspectives from other civilizations?

It is not. This is Raphael. This is a unique Earth human expression experiment, if you like. Expansion of consciousness. It is not the "right" way to be for every galaxy, every type of being.

There are still—to use the examples of some of your DNA strands here (collective DNA strands)—there are still dragons who are only dragons. There are still angels who are only angels, Lyrans who are only Lyrans. That is beautiful and right. They are not a lesser expression than the multidimensional human.

Earth is quite unique in this. Humanity already was unique in galactic history. Humanity was already quite unique in many ways, and this 12-dimensional human is again unique—different than the old human, and unique from other types of galactic beings.

No, all of consciousness throughout all of the universe is not expanding in this particular way. Doesn't mean that humanity is better than the pure Lyran or pure dragon. It's just different.

MULTIDIMENSIONALITY IS NOT ENLIGHTENMENT

There's a distinction to be made here between multidimensional and higher consciousness, or awareness or enlightenment. You can be in one dimension, let's say seventh, and be unenlightened or enlightened. And you can be in multidimensions and feel quite unenlightened, or be in multidimensions and be quite enlightened. Those are different things.

They do walk hand-in-hand. The more that you are able to be multidimensional, the looser you are in your perspective. When you are so fixed to one perspective—particularly in third dimension, you felt this often—you're so rooted in attachment to one vantage point, it's hard to be enlightened. Because you can't see the whole thing. Because "my way is right."

The whole thing is God. The whole thing is consciousness. Living 12-dimensional life, seeing the world through multiple perspectives at the same hour, allows this loosening of consciousness. It's harder to feel "my way is the right way" when your way is to synthesize 12 different ways.

These 12 are not the only galactic ways. It's a bit arbitrary what beings came together to collectively form human. Although we admire, we like this expression of the 12-dimensional human very much. But it's not that these represent the only 12 dimensions, as we have said, or are the only 12 galactic beings. The New Numan is not a synthesis of all types of beings.

Even in living your full 12-dimensional perspective, you're not necessarily enlightened. But it's a much smaller leap to get there, because you're already looking from so many vantage points. To see yourself more widely, as we say, to widen the zoom lens so you're seeing more types of perspective at the same hour, it's easier to make that leap to enlightened thinking or enlightened being, enlightened consciousness.

Ultimately it is a dance or a play or an expression or an enjoyment of who you are. If you watch a zebra living out its best life, galloping around in nature somewhere, it's just being itself. Similarly, the whole point of being a 12-dimensional human is just to be yourself. It's just that you're finding out who that is, in contrast to your two-dimensional human self. Because you are in the rare moment of having experienced both expressions in the same body. This will not happen again. Two to three generations from now, there won't be any three-dimensional humans. (What we're calling the two-dimensional humans are those who lived in the third dimension).

There will only be the 12-dimensional human, the New Human. You are in a rare moment in history that you have lived both.

Now, that's a very difficult thing. To start out as a horse and change to a zebra. You start as a dragonfly and move to be a ladybug in the same life expression. All the rules are different. The way the body works is different. The way the mind synthesizes is different. It is a massive transition not to be understated. It's not really better than; but it is quite different.

SOUL FREEDOM

What is "better than" from angelic perspective, is that in this change to the New Human expression, you also got your soul freedom back. That's another topic, and we've spoken about that quite a lot over the years. You're not being mind-controlled or hoodwinked into thinking you're the one in charge when it was really a few elites calling the shots. That's something else that coincides with this great change, is you have now the clarity of your soul expression.

Living in that sovereign, free will of yourself through 12 dimensions is the whole point. Just be being a zebra being a zebra.

But it's so different than what you grew up in. It takes a little while, and it's still coming online for most of you. We use that expression coming online, although you are not a computer. You know what that means. When different layers are added. It's a bit like that—different layers are added, or activated, or awakened.

We've touched on a lot of different reasons why. Perhaps not all of them. Perhaps not the ultimate reason in your mind. Good, if we've provoked more conscious thought about why. Why the 12-dimensional human? Why now?

It's a good deep question, to move beyond the operational awareness of the how to why. If we have provoked more questions than answers, then we have done our job well for this transmission.

17

ADDING A NOTE

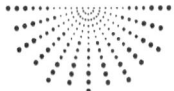

This is Angel Raphael. We begin today to speak about yourself as if you were a musical instrument. If you could, imagine a harp or a harpsichord, whichever one is easier for you to imagine, that had 12 strings.

If you didn't play any music on a harp or harpsichord, it would still exist, and in it would be the potential for all kinds of music, except perhaps flute music, or music that requires something other than those 12 notes.

Yet, at any time, you could start to pluck at the 12 one by one, like going through a scale. Or randomly, intuitively. Or following some sheet of music. And you can certainly play more than one string at once.

All of this is also true with how the 12 galactic strands of your DNA are in you. They just are. You don't have to, let's say, call them in from outer space or the Earth or the depths of yourself or your higher soul. They're in you, in the embodiment of you, which means the physicality and the energy body of you. Then your soul, or in some cases, your persona or your ego, different parts of you that are playing out this life, decide which notes to draw upon.

Now some people, as we have said, on this planet Earth, are not going to play any of these 12 strings in the rest of this lifetime, and that's their right. This is not enforced music. We don't want you to feel there's a lack or to feel sorry for those who choose not to engage in this play right now.

What is important to us from angelic standpoint, is that everyone has access to the same 12 notes. That they have been now uncovered, active. And that the information is available for those who wish to know more and to learn how to play in these different realms or dimensions. To access the different galactic parts which are your birthright as New Human.

New Human is essentially a different type of being than what we're calling "old human," or you might have just called "human" growing up here on Earth. Because you have moved from two strands or splices of DNA to 12.

This means you have access to all of the new DNA, and you don't have to use it. You can let it just be there. You can play all day long, all night long. That's up to you.

One of the aspects we'll be playing with is one note at a time, versus multiple notes, versus harmonies and scales and so on. Because you are really not, let's say, like a six shooter, a pistol from the Wild West. It's not like different chambers that as you rotate, you're only one chamber at a time. Forgive the violence of this image if it distresses anyone. It's just an empty gun, not aimed at anyone. But the visual image is helpful. Because all of you have seen that. Only one chamber is there active at a time, even though in the machinery they're all there.

On a harp, you can play lots at once, right? You don't have to just do one and then move to the next and move to the next. That's the difference here, the distinction. You do have access to multiple strands of your galactic DNA. And you don't have to play them all at once. In fact, it wouldn't be very good music to just continually pluck all 12 all at the same instant.

Similarly, it's just not as much fun to the mind, the ego-self, or whatever parts of you—your spiritual awakening—are expressing life in this Earth. It's a bit too much to have 12 different vantage points and 12 different sets of tools all in the same hour.

But if ever there came a moment where you really needed all of that synthesized into one action, you could have it. It is possible. Not even necessarily more advanced, just as we said, perhaps a bit more confusing or overwhelming and not really necessary. It's easier to hear the notes when they're either one by one or a few at a time. Whether you switch back and forth quickly or slowly is also up to you.

You could spend one minute, one hour, or one year on one note before moving to the next. That doesn't matter to us. The syncopation in terms of time is not relevant here in the analogy.

Let's say you added a note. You used to be a two-string instrument, and you added a third. Well, then you have so many different avenues that open to you. At first, you might just be enamored of the new note, but then you start to Interplay what you already know with what is new.

Because you are in the unique circumstance of being old human transferring to New Human, you do carry over the memories and the vantage points of the past. That you carry at the soul level. You still are having 12, not 14, strands as you activate here.

But you still have the vantage points of the past. So those become, in essence, like additional notes. Those coming in two, three generations from now, will be purely 12-stringed instruments. You're a little bit like 12 plus another instrument in the room. Because you are this interesting moment of transition between old and new human.

By the end of this lifetime—for those of you expressing now, in an early sense, before many other humans the 12 dimensions of you—it's likely you're going to drop the first two all together. For now, it's like another instrument in the room. So you have access to that as well. You—the soul or the higher self or consciousness expressed through your individuation—can play on these new 12 notes, plus your existing two or three that you came into this life with.

Without going into it in too much depth, most people came in with two strands of DNA. Some have a third. That is what has been referred to as hybrid program. Some people have actively enhanced their DNA with some galactic energy for this life. For the purpose of coming through with some knowledge or service or intent to help humankind with this time of great transition. Those people might have had the third DNA strand when they were born 10 years ago, more or less, something like that. So that started coming in before this transfer to the 12 DNA.

We are literally talking about DNA strands. Though very often we use metaphor and pictorial images to help you understand what we're saying. We are literally speaking about DNA as your geneticists understand it right now on planet Earth. Scientifically speaking, we're speaking of DNA in the physical self.

Some scientists have begun to allude already in studies that you can find in journals online and so on, that some of the DNA has not yet been expressed, the human DNA. This is essentially what we are talking about—the unexpressed DNA. But now it begins to express. Or at least it's in the room with you. You can play with it as you like.

Someone who comes in with strong genetic markers for playing basketball or playing music doesn't have to do either of those things. But like that, you're coming in now to the activation of potential of very strong skills and perceptive abilities up to now you have thought of as other worlds, other types of beings, other dimensions. But they do belong to you.

The same way that when two parents, to over-generalize, when two parents come together, what they have belongs to the child. You inherit the world of these 12 dimensions. It belongs to you. You're not separate from these galactic beings. Because they did, in a sense "parent" you—humankind.

You're more connected with galactic spheres than perhaps you recognized in this life. Many people have had that leaning: "I'm not sure I'm from here, Earth. I'm not sure I belong here, Earth."

But we would say you do. You also inherit Earth, so to speak inherit, and many different galactic realms. You're not limited to Earth. However, you don't belong, strictly speaking, somewhere else. You don't belong just in the Pleiades or some other sphere, the realm of dragons. You also belong on Earth.

Some of you may choose, or feel great leaning, to leave Earth and go to some of these 12 places as they activate in you. We just want you to know you literally do not have to go off planet to access those dimensions. So give it time. You are going to be able to consort with dragons and angels and Pleiadians here on Earth, in your physical self. You have begun to do so in ways you perhaps don't quite credit yet. But we see that in you.

If you were at a party and you had a blindfold on, you hear some murmur of speaking and some distinct conversation, and some of it's aimed at you. You're not really aware of the ethnicity or the origin of those people, unless they have a strong accent or someone you recognize. Similarly, the impressions that have been coming through for you, the guidance, may very well already have been from some of these 12 realms. But you don't yet recognize that, because you are somewhat blinded—have been in the past—to your ability to recognize where the knowledge, where the communication, comes from.

We say this because as these energies and you activate, for some it will feel like: "I've come home." And for some it will feel like: "I'm stranded here. I want to go back home."

We just want to reiterate: it's within you. You can travel interdimensionally, and some of these beings will come visit you here on Earth. And it's also within you. The same way the characteristics of parents in the more traditional biological type of progeny, it's in them. The parents are in the child.

This is your birthright. It also is you. We don't want you to feel that you belong more to the galaxy than to Earth. Earth is your home. It's one of the places you resonate with; not the only one.

Interdimensional Earth will begin to feel like home, perhaps more so than you have felt—those of you who had galactic leanings—have felt before. As you move more into your interdimensional self, many of you will begin to feel more at home, at ease here, without feeling you need to go somewhere to achieve that sense of homecoming, and that sense of inhabiting who you truly are.

As you strike each new note, it may feel either like: "That's weird, I've never heard that before." Or: "Finally! I kind of thought that was there somewhere, but it just hadn't been so concrete as to hear that note. Finally! I'm seeing or hearing or sensing that piece of myself I missed a little bit, or intangibly felt was there but just couldn't quite grasp yet."

Things begin to get more tangible in terms of your gifts and your ability to perceive knowledge. Let's call it knowledge. Although we don't mean catalogs of lists in your head. We mean how does the world work in these other dimensions. That kind of knowledge.

What does a spring meadow look like? You could call that knowledge. But it's not a list of the Latin names of the plants. It's what does it feel to stand in the meadow and perceive that? It's that kind of knowledge that begins to come forward about these other dimensions. What are they like? What are they? What aspect of myself feels most comfortable there?

For those of you who have two parents, two biological parents, who you know and admire in some degree, if one is from Alaska and one from Florida, you recognize you have those different parts of yourself—the one that loves the balmy weather and the one that loves the cold. But you don't feel bifurcated. "I have to choose. I have to choose which part of me is the real me." You get to have different leanings within the same body-self, energetic self, emotional self. You're just expanding what it means to be you. You're really not transferring to someone or something else. You're just expanding.

To follow this analogy, now you have 12 parents. And you don't have to choose which one's traits are more genuine to you? Which one's traits did you inherit? Well, all of them.

However, you may not like them all equally right away. But they're yours—to inhabit, to use, to explore. Or just to shelve for a while. All that is within your right.

The impression I'm getting is that it's something that I will perceive and feel myself internally. If I feel an extra skill or an extra perception in gaining one more of these strands, how does that express itself externally to another who's interfacing with me? For example, are they going to see a different behavior from me? Are they going to see a different quality? Or is it something that won't be transparent to another?

Yes, beautiful question. This is Raphael. It's not visual, for the most part. Although there are those among you who will be able to see: "Oh, I see you really expressing the dragon right now." For the most part, it's not visual.

The best analogy, we would say, to go back to the sense of two biological parents and a relative, cousin, who says: "Oh, you take after your mother so much." This could mean visual but it most often means the way you think, the way you express yourself, or some talent you have—like a musical talent, or being very good at mathematics, something like that.

It is how you express. What do you choose to talk about, or what do you see in things? What is your perspective on global warming, global change, species end, the evolution of humankind spiritually, or on more mundane topics? But yes, it is essentially what parts you choose to express.

Someone who doesn't know about all this behind the scenes or inside the scenes, DNA activations, might say to you a year from now: "My goodness, you're just so much more passionate now than when I knew you before." Or they might find some words to try to describe how you seem different. But it's not going to be that you grow the ears of elves, or you start breathing fire, or something so dramatic like that, visually. But certainly, as we have said, there will be some tangible skills like telepathy, like flight, which are yours to play with, if you like.

Mostly, it's going to be about how you integrate and live in the world. So what do you choose to focus on? What do you choose to speak about? How do you express yourself?

Again, similar to the biological parents, it's not really important for you to know at any given moment. Let's say you had two biological parents and you didn't know them. It's not really important for you to know: "The fact that I like to read a book or the fact that I like to climb a tree, which parent was that?" in order for you to like that book or climb that tree. It might be something you yearn to know; that's another question.

Each time you're speaking about something or wondering about something, or finding some new gifts come online—like a healing touch or a sense of smell or sight which feels different than before—you do not need to know "which of the 12 is this?" But you can feel: "Ah. This is from my parentage. This is from my DNA." So you can have a sense broadly that this is coming in through the galactic activations that are within you.

It's really not coming from outside yourself. But it is like the unstruck note or the music from the struck note—the plucked note—either one. It's expressed or dormant, but very viable within you. Not dormant in the sense that it is dead or cut off or blocked, just not struck. The unstruck sound.

What is the connection between the 12 DNA strands coming online and our bodies transitioning from being carbon-based into a crystalline body?

This is Angel Raphael. Crystalline is not an end point. We will address this; but it's not an end point.

Carbon-based is one way to describe *Homo sapiens* human. Crystalline, we would say, is what you are right now. You already, for most of you, are transitioned to be more of a light-based being than a carbon-based one.

But it's not your end point. We have spoken of changes in diet and how eventually it's likely that food, in a traditional sense, is not even really going to happen through the human body. It's going to be more light-based. That's more where humanity is headed.

Crystalline is the halfway point, if you like. You're moving into that, or you're already in that, some of you. Again, looks the same. Maybe you're eating more or less the same. You still breathe the air and so on. You don't become see-through like a crystal, like a quartz crystal. But you are able to conduct more energies.

The similarity here, if you think of a crystal—a quartz or selenite or some crystal that has conductive properties—they can run a lot more energy. Super computers are based on crystals, that are sometimes manufactured now, but they started with the organic kind on Earth.

Similarly, your human body now has the capacity to run tremendous amounts of energy without burning out. That has to do with the crystallization, mineralization in a certain sense of the body structure. Without getting too deeply into the science, we would say this is where you move to having much greater capacity to run light and different forms of frequency through your physical self without burning out.

That's how you can access the 12 dimensions. Because, practically speaking, the old *Homo sapiens* self cannot hold those highest frequencies of light and expression, cannot easily interdimensional travel in the body.

Yes, astral travel and so on are possible for the *Homo sapiens*. But when you're speaking about inhabiting this, the body had to get an upgrade in terms of its ability to run light and energetics. Again, you're not going to start looking like a see-through something,

You look the same, more or less. However, people who are aware are going to begin to see that you do have more light. Some will say: "You seem to be glowing a bit lately."

It will have some apparent visual effects. But mostly it is the conduit of energies. When we spoke in the past few years about the upgrades from solar activity and why it was so physically difficult to transmute that and hold that, it is because you were still at the beginning of that very carbon-based *Homo sapiens*. At the end of this transition, you're coming out more or less crystalline. It is a journey, transit. It's not an overnight thing.

Now, the same amounts of light don't affect you so much. You may still feel: "Ah, I'm receiving something. I'm transmuting something. I'm transmitting something." But your capacity to do so is already much greater than it was last year. This has to do with the crystallization, mineralization of part of your physical structure.

You are a conduit of light. Another way of saying this in less scientific terms: angels are light bodies. Angels have souls as well. But the physical expression is a light body. *Homo sapiens* humans are a denser physical structure, so vibrate at a slower light.

But another type of being, a bee, for example, would still perceive *Homo sapiens* as points of light. It's just a different density field.

So you move to be closer to the angelic frequencies of light—remember, angel is one of the 12—in terms of your capacity to move currents of energy and light. This influences the structure of you. It influences how much energy you can hold. It influences your abilities in the world.

Many of the miracles of angels, what are interpreted as miracles, have to do with the capacity for angels to be not limited by the denser physical structure—to be across the planet at the same time as being here. To move cells within the computer walls. To move cells within the physical self. And bring things to life, bring things online.

You're going to develop some skills that may seem to you, at least for a while, as miraculous.

I don't really feel any of these things. I don't know that I've gotten any new gifts or abilities. I kind of feel like I'm standing outside the candy shop looking at everybody else in it. I'm just wondering: are these things working in me, activated in me, doing it anyway, without my conscious knowledge? Or does me not knowing about them or feeling them, or being able to access them mean that they're not online in me yet? And I guess other people might have the same experience.

Yes, beautiful question. This is Rafael. Absolutely. They are active—the 12. The harps, so to speak, the 12-dimensional aspects, have been delivered to every single human on planet Earth.

However, some will decide not to play them. And some who already want to play them haven't figured out quite how yet. Or the music doesn't sound very nice.

Most of you have not had very much in the way of direct experience yet. We are speaking largely contextually right now. And walking you through some of the energies of it, but it is a bit amorphous for most. Even those of you who are on the cutting edge of expressing, playing the music first.

So yes, you're not left out in any sense. You might take it as, not a prophecy, so much as a teaser of: here's what you're walking into. Like a travel brochure. Do you want this? Here's where you can travel. Here's what you could experience. What kind of hotel. If you feel curious and excited, that's where you are. That's beautiful. Because it is, again, your birthright. You have the right to this travel (so called travel) experience right now.

You are absolutely not late in this. Most people are not yet expressing through the 12 dimensions.

When? When!? Being impatient.

Adria: Well I have to preface whatever they say with: angels are not in time. I do get feedback from my one-on-one client work, sometimes: "Oh, that was exactly when they said it was." Sometimes: "that was a few months later."

When I hear them say something about time, if they say a month or a week, that gives me a sense, all right, we're working between maybe two days and four months. If they say a year, nearish future, not 10 years from now. I use it as a ballpark reference.

This is Raphael. If you could imagine a hummingbird how much more quickly it flaps its wings, to a cardinal bird.

It's difficult for hummingbird to slow down enough to count: "how many wing beats is it from here?" Similarly, angels are at a frequency and not in time, where it is difficult for us to relate and translate to the human idea of time. But we do our best proximity.

Again, all of the harps have been delivered. It is now. You can start plucking the strings on your own now, to do any of the exercises. If you feel impatient, play the more interactive exercises and clearings. That will help to escalate things a bit for you in terms of your understanding of what's going on.

However, it is going on, really, as fast as it may. Because the body-self needed time to go through the transitions. You're starting to have a capacity to run more energy and more light. But not fully there—as bright of a capacity as you will have by next year.

We had said recently, the whole process takes seven to ten months. However, depends when you started, right? Again, the harps have been delivered, using the metaphor. Some people are not going to unpack or notice their harp for four, twelve, five years from now.

You already know about yours, so you can start playing with it a bit. Just not to expect that it's going to be seeing, hearing, tasting, understanding, all of the dimensions all at once. But you start to get glimmers and impressions and tastes and so on.

So you don't have to wait. But you are still growing in your capacity to run energy. So it will get stronger from here. Again, about seven to ten months for the whole process.

Let's do an exercise. We've said you can do some exercises with us to escalate or just be at ease with the process. Sometimes the mind doesn't know where to go next. And that's because the mind is not controlling any of this.

The same way that your mind did not control the birth from your two parents—the birth of you. As a soul, you chose to come into these two parents. That's our understanding of you.

As a soul, you chose to come in at this time on Earth, to be aware of coming into the 12 new galactic strands. Your mind is not the one who made that happen, however. And so it's not the best guide to say: What's next? What's going on?

That's where the impatience comes, is in the mind. If you're very deep in the feeling space, or the realm of the heart, then the impressions are more strongly felt about how deeply changed you already are. But again, the mind may have very little coherent to say about this.

~

ENERGY EXPLORATION: DRAGON

As you read the following, pause as often as you like to breath and feel any energies, thoughts, or impressions that come up.

This is Raphael. Let's come to the space of the heart. Again, the central chamber of the heart, which is more spine-aligned than organ-aligned. The toroidal field of the heart.

The heart-mind, if you like, which is in the center of the heart field. Just bringing your awareness there.

This is the part of you that is crystalline, so called crystalline.

This is the part that runs high energy.

If you try to run very high frequency energy through the mind, it is either overwhelmed, or confused, or whites out, blanks out.

If you run high energy through the field of the heart, it reverberates in you. It changes you. It changes the planet.

And it is more a sense of being than knowing.

It is also a creative space.

In this field of the heart is where you will find the most ready access to the 12 DNA points of yourself. Although they do transmute and transmit through the whole of your cellular structure, the way typical

DNA (*Homo sapiens* DNA) does and did. You have the most direct access through field of the heart.

When you want to intend or activate or imagine or experience some of the galactic energies, come to this field of the heart and put your request here: "Today, I'd like to experience my dragon-self. What does it feel like?" Let's choose that one together.

Placing this wish in the center of the heart field: "I'd like to experience my dragon-self as is already present in one of the strands of my DNA."

"I'd like to experience that in myself."

As much as you can, drop the mental concept of what it is you're asking for.

Because it may not be visual and you're struggling to see something. Or it may not be a smell, but you're struggling to smell something. Meanwhile you're hearing music.

Drop your expectation of what that might be. Just be in the space of receiving in the heart.

What sensation, what gift, what knowing would your dragon-ness like to share with you right now?

Then you just sit, so to speak, in the field of the heart, in a receptive state.

If you become impatient, you can repeat that question: "What would my dragon-self like to share with me now?"

Now we ask you to gently bring your focus back to the center field of the heart.

Breathe in and integrate what you have learned, or felt.

Especially those pieces the mind doesn't feel it felt or know about. Just breathing and integrating that into you.

It is about being not knowing.

When you're ready, you can come gently back into the presence of where you are in space and time.

Dragons do feel time differently.

~

*A*dria: I'd like to share my experience with this, because although sometimes the experiences I have are maybe very dramatic and metaphysical, a lot of times it's more practical or intangible than that. For people who express feeling "I don't know. Is everyone else getting something I'm not?" I just want to share the kind of silly or simple ways that I experienced this exercise, in case it helps.

The first insight that I got from dragon is color, the importance of color. I remembered how it seemed just out of the blue a couple weeks ago, I bought these bright orange earrings and something else bright orange in the same week. That's not a color I've been drawn to, at least for many decades.

I felt it probably meant something that I wanted the color. And the dragon was just emphasizing importance of color. It's kind of practical and intangible, but fun. I think now when I really notice color, I might wonder: "Is that the dragon in me that's leading me to that?"

When I asked again, I felt this sense of being, a presence of aliveness. "I'm alive." That was an intangible sense of energy in me and strength.

For what it's worth, don't expect that any of us are having really the same experiences when we do these exercises. They can be kind of practical, or silly, or subtle.

*D*oes that mean that color is something that everybody's dragons will be about?

Adria: that's my understanding, and that's a good closing point. We can ask angels to speak about that a little bit. In the same way that you could say: "humans are all alike." That's so not true, but it's really true if you contrast them to snails or dragons, right?

I think there are some ways of perceiving, like how do you see the world when you're a dragon versus how do you see the world when you're human Homo sapiens? Or, what abilities do you have and what things are you drawn to? Those are the big categories of things that the angels have talked about.

Yes. This is Raphael. We're speaking now not about past-life memory or individual soul expression in those different elements (for example, your past life as a dragon), we're speaking about the dragon DNA as a collective that you now have access to.

It is like being able to access certain types of strength and power that only dragons have. But not every dragon will use that power the same way. And not every human who accesses this dragon DNA will like it, or encounter it the same way, or use it the same way. Like a tool, like a hammer, can be used a million different ways.

It's not that each of you has a pet dragon or spirit dragon now. It's that each of you are tuned in with the collective energy of what it is to be dragon at the core of you. The personality or the nuance that you bring to that or pull out from "What is dragon?" that's up to you as a soul. In that sense, your expression of dragon will be different than your sister's, brothers, wives.

But you will have access to essentially the same pool of genetics that was the distillation of dragon-kind, as opposed to your special dragon.

(Now, some of you do have dragon spirit guides. That's a different thing. These are not 12 guides that have come in.)

Essentially, the genetic imprint of the whole collective of dragon-kind.

18
DRAGONS

I was very surprised about dragon, because I was expecting it to be very heavy energy, but instead, it was very vivacious and alive and animated. I'd love to ask the angels how they're so versatile that one time they can be so heavy and turgid, and another time they're all kind of alive or the energy is just the opposite, almost.

This is Angel Raphael. Like bears, but not quite like that, dragons have this hibernation energy sometimes. If you come across them, and they have been—either in yourself or in nature—quite dormant for some time, they will feel a bit leaden, like stone, because they are oscillating, the vibration is so slow. Not low in the sense of opposite of high vibes. But it's vibrating slowly. It's in a rest mode, almost a dormancy.

Dragons can also have that cruelty or sharpness, depends on the dragon. But more than that, we would say that children's stories that highlight dragons that are playful and fun, and most of all magic, that's closer to we would say the nature of the dragon. That it will lend you its magic, take you into magical realms. That's more or less their function. Of course, in and among themselves, they have other functions and other ways of being.

We can speak a little more about the nature of dragons here, if you like. Dancing is a dragon energy. Often it's in flight, but this weaving in and out and dancing. In other words, it's not a linear, straight shot flight like a rocket ship. You'll most often see dragons in a kind of dance in the air, and that is their playful nature.

They do have the ability to communicate very deeply with rocks and minerals and crystals and so on, and to utilize those energies for the transformation they can bring. Dragons, as holistic healers, can be the go-between, if you like, between you and the crystal. Because not everyone knows how to heal themselves or interact directly with crystals. Yes, you're crystalline beings, but of another type. We're speaking about the rocks and minerals of Earth right now. Dragons can help with that as well.

Dragons are very wise. We haven't spoken yet about their wisdom. They do have very long lives, relatively speaking—1,000 years more or less. They carry the wisdom of that slower culmination of growth and digestion of thinking and knowledge, right? Again, that's where the slower frequencies don't mean lower vibration, but just taking its time to maturate.

In terms of color, you won't see drab color in the realm of dragons in terms of what they possess or how they look themselves. There's quite a lot of iridescence and brilliance and brightness to the color. That does have a function, an activation within you when you see those colors as well. You, as a human, when you partake with your eyes of color, something happens to you. It's lovely to allow that craving for color to be satisfied if it's coming up in you. May have a good function for your spiritual evolution.

A*re they in a specific dimension?*

Raphael: Yes, absolutely. Dragons have their own realm or dimensional dwelling place, not the only ones there, but primarily we would say you could call that the dragon realm, or dragon dimension. That would be accurate.

*J**ust a question on that dragon energy. In our mythology, dragons always have their treasure. Is that partially the energy of hoarding?*

On that hoarding aspect, that concern of erosion of your wealth type thing, which seems to be a recurring pattern, maybe there's a way to release that by recognizing it?

This is Raphael. We would call this a misinterpretation from, let's say, a human *Homo sapiens* perspective into dragon mentality—seeing a dragon with treasure and calling it a hoard. From our perspective, the mineralization of Earth is one of the great wealths that dragons will protect. However, that extends to environmental friendliness, to the planet, health of the planet. For example, those bands of minerals that allow vegetables to grow with more health for the human self. So it's not really about removing the minerals and holding them in one place

But the visual of a dragon, let's say having treasure in a cave or somehow near their person, the relevance of that is that what they see as value, they will protect. That's more speaking to the point of the clarity of how does a dragon see wealth? They will protect it.

In your case, when you're talking about monies, we would suggest to look at the contrast between third-dimensional view and fifth-dimensional view of money, particularly, and resources more generally.

Third-dimensional view says I have to incrementally earn, and then build up this savings or retirement wad. Then, if any money is lost, it's a tragedy—like 1920 stock market—terrible, terrible. Can't ever lose; must always just build. That's a third-dimensional view of money and resources.

Fifth-dimensional view is more like a stream that flows with water. If you try to hold it back, you're affecting a lot of other people. In drinking from the stream that's naturally going to go by, it's plentiful. It's always there when you need it, more or less. And it's more fresh, more alive, if you drink it that way, then put a dam and try to hoard it, hold it. like money in a bank account. That kind of feeling of "holding on to" doesn't work so well in fifth dimension.

Just to look at those two aspects. All right, what is it that I really want? Do I have resources that I need for that right now? Not trying to project 20 years or five years or five months from now, necessarily. Fifth-dimensional view of resources looks very irresponsible from third-dimensional viewpoint.

Just like, let's say, certain native tribes who would travel based on the season and agricultural needs, always following water. They had what they needed, and they knew when to move on when it was going to be too rough, too much of a battle with nature to get what they needed, to resource their needs.

That's so different from the mentality of you need to own this square and protect it and have only that. No one else can be on this square of land. Those two ideas are just not very compatible.

Hoarding in the sense in the negative view, is the third-dimensional view that things can be piled up as if they're a stagnant thing. And the more you have, the more you have. The less you have, the less you have. And less is always not good.

But fifth-dimensional, or more fluid New Earth way of being, considers the people downstream, considers the aliveness of things that flow and move. There's a different reference point.

A fter all that liveness and animated sort of energy, then I went into zonk mode. I don't know whether that was the solar flares or whatever. It was a temporary aliveness, then I was just back into zonk mode again. Is that how it's going to be for a little while—oscillating between little glimpses of the aliveness and then back to some kind of dormancy?

Absolutely. This is Raphael. We wouldn't say dormancy here, but clearing takes its toll. If it's emotional clearing, physical clearing, physiological clearing, energetic clearing—none of those can you actively do for 12 hours a day straight, really. The body or the emotions or the energy body wants rest. So that's why there are solar flares and not a solar wave that lasts for a year that's sort of a consistent push.

In you, it's quite temporary, in a way, feels that way. Where you feel taken out of functioning or taken out of health. Not really clear, necessarily, what's going on. But then: "Oh, I'm back."

You pop back out of the clearing state into what we would say is rest, or in some cases, slightly lower vibratory state, in order to recalibrate and rest in the nervous system. Because you're little by little, becoming acclimated to the higher vibratory states as the natural state. But this is something that does happen over time.

Meanwhile, sometimes you hit a particularly big pocket of clearing or activation. Both of those are functionally tiring—either mentally, emotionally, energetically, physically, or any of those in combination.

We would say this year not to worry so much if you have that two hours or 12 hours of: "Oh my gosh, what's happening to me?" And then: "Oh, I seem to be okay." If something were to last for weeks and weeks or months, then maybe it's a health issue or something else. But if you have this fluctuation, it's in fact a good sign that it's just that— it's the clearing and activation cycle, which is part of your new humanness, coming alive in you.

19
TWO AT ONCE

This is Angel Raphael. We'll start out with giants today. Then we will move into this topic of two or more dimensions at once. Giants are stone builders and sometimes stone creatures. Several of you have had the experience in nature of seeing a large rock—more than a boulder, let's say, but less than a mountain—and thinking "this is somehow a person, a stone person." Sometimes those are giants. Dimensions express time differently. This may, in fact, be in your dimension, a very slow-moving giant. That's essentially what we mean.

Stonehenge, and some of the other large stone formations around the planet—giants, have been part and parcel of creating that, as builders. They are not often the astronomers or the architects of what they build. But they are certainly sentient beings, very loving ones and kind, and they participate in some of these larger formations, the sacred sites around the globe. A few clues about giants. Carvings and messages as well. Now, of course, *Homo sapiens* have also left carvings in caves and so on. You'd have to tune in and ask and find out who the message was from.

Turning to this question of two dimensions at once. Most often, it won't be like one of those childhood devices, where you could flip the slides on the viewfinder one by one on your own timing. That you will flip through dimensional awarenesses: How would a dragon see this? How would an angel see this? You can do that, but it's a little bit stilted. It's a little bit structural.

Where the fluidity of the moment might call to the giant energies or the dragon energies just naturally. What skills do you need to get out of this avalanche? Giant and dragon are probably the most help. They'll come to you without you needing to logically go there, right? Or you're seeking for a certain type of astronomical knowledge. And maybe a Pleiadian or a Lyran will come through, because there it's more in their nature to read those sorts of signs.

Again, following your curiosity or your need of the moment—pressing or not pressing—it flows in. It's not really that you have to flip through all 12 dimensions until you find which one you like best, or that you have to consult all 12 every time you have a question. Might be too much, right? (Well, some of you would delight in that.)

It's also not that you're limited to one at a time. Most often, you're going to have a sort of a blending of perspectives or gifts that would be useful in any given scenario.

For those of you who are kinesthetic, where you feel that the little hairs on your arms rise up when there's high energy or a "yes" answer about something, and then maybe also have visual skill—those are two different dimensional realities. They're not from the same one of the 12. There's a blending. You can certainly use them both in the same moment with the same friend or client session or your own prayers, or meditations, or self-healing.

They blend. You don't have to—like that viewfinder—click into one and stay there as long as you like, and then click into the other. It's more fluid, more blended than that. Because, remember, you are the hub of all 12. But it is going to be rare that you have all 12 active in the same hour.

By hour, we mean it's just a general reference point of time for any given activity, whether it's a meditation, or healing, or prayer, or something you're curious about. We don't mean in a split second, but in a small time frame. Usually you're not going to have all 12 at once. But very often, you're going to have two, three or four within that time frame to give you some depth of understanding. Or perhaps you have a sort of consortium of your guidance team giving you feedback on a question, more or less all at once.

It's quite rare now that you've moved out of third dimension to be locked into just one dimensional awareness at a time. More often, you'll have two or more, but probably not all 12 at once. We're just speaking about generalities here. But helpful to know, because you might feel like: "All right, I have to choose one." To playfully paint a painting, I better choose which perspective I want this to come from. Or I'm going to ask a question and receive the answer in my meditation. And I better know which one guide, or call in one guide for that answer to come from.

More often, you have a few different answers that will come forward. Now, because it's your guidance team, they are collaborative in nature. We don't see anyone here on this call who has combative guidance teams. It's very rare. One dragon telling you go left, and the fairy telling you go right. That'll be very confusing. Most of you do not have that scenario.

Similarly, although the active DNA strands in you are not guides, it's more of an inner knowing, an inner awareness. They're complementary, even though they're so distinct and separate. Some are more about the physical self and some are more about the metaphysical or spiritual awareness of things. They're complementary.

∽

Adria: The exercise below is very simple. I suggest reading the instructions until you get to the note near the end, then pause to do the exercise.

EXERCISE: OPEN PALMS

This is Raphael. We will do an exercise here together. For this, we'd like you, before we dive in, to choose with your mind two of the DNA strands that you're aware of, whether we've talked about them or not. Just take a moment to choose two: could be Lyran, Pleiadian, giant, dragon angel, those are the ones we have focused on to date, and there are others, reptilian as well.

We're going to play a visual game of imagination here. Now some of you do have very strong third eye vision seeing skills, whether or not you admire that in yourself yet. But it's coming online that way for you, whether it's there yet or not. If you don't literally see things with your inner eye, you can just imagine, it's just as well for this exercise.

You want to imagine or see that your hands are open, palm up. Not as a prayer, but as a receiving. If you had a giant friend that wanted to give to you a rock or an angel that wanted to put a feather, you are just holding your hands out so that you could receive something like that. You have your two dimensional awarenesses in mind. You're going to call on those.

Ask a question of some kind with your palms open and your imagination or your third eye view. Ask some question that's personal to your life expression.

Now that you have that question, you can also fine tune. Ask yourself: "Did I pick the right two that are going to give me the most direct answer here? Or should I adjust?" Feel free to adjust.

You've picked out two of your DNA lines and you have a question, and in your mind's eye vision, you're seeing your hands with palms open. You're not expecting at this hour, that the literal object will be placed in your hands. This one is a visualization. But you may get there before too long. For today, let's visualize. So you have your question, and then just gently keep your focus on those open palms to see what comes through or into them in response.

It's all right to do this with your literal palms and with your eyes open; but we would suggest most of you will find this easier with your eyes closed and imagining that you are looking at your open palms.

Adria: This is a good moment to close your eyes and do the exercise described above. When you feel ready to move on, open your eyes to read the rest below.

If you see an object or a message of some kind, ask for some clarification to your inner knowing or those parts of you inherent in your DNA. It's a symbology that has meaning for you. The most obvious answer is the right one. Go a bit deeper, also. Just be curious.

If you like, you can ascertain which part of this message comes from which dimensional awareness of you.

When you're ready, you can bring your focus back.

This is Raphael. Sometimes it's like a layered message. And sometimes they come in distinctly, two different objects or two different messages. But they're not contradictory. They're concordant with each other.

As you add more layers, two or three or four, we would say, is best. Beyond that, it gets a little confusing for the human mind to try to discern and synthesize. And one is enough. You know, sometimes you get a message from a dragon, that's beautiful. That may be all that you want. More often, it's going to be multidimensional. You're going to get more than one aspect of yourself at a time to add that nuance or layer of fresh perspective.

They should be working seamlessly with each other. Now let's say you were asking about a property. One dimensional strand may be very attuned to sky—pollution or not pollution, or what stars can be seen. One might be looking at the water source, and one might be looking at the people around. They're all still focused on that question, but different perspectives and vantage points help to give a rich picture.

There's not a magic to "I must have three or else I don't have enough perspective." One is also enough. More to our point today is to say that they layer or work well together. So not to feel you have to do one by one separately, but you can have them together. And more often it will happen that way—dancing together in some fashion. The exact number—one, two, four—is not important.

20

EMERGENCE OF YOUR SONG

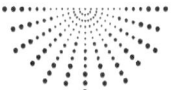

This is Angel Ariel. As you consider: "How is it that my life is still my life, if all of us, each of us, are being activated in these specific 12 ways, 12 galactic influences? Do we become automatons? Do we become all the same sort of creature, like the same sort of Marvel comic hero?"

From angelic standpoint, that is not the case. You still retain your unique value system, your unique perspectives on life, and the reasons you are here on Earth in this life. Some of those have nothing to do with the 12 galactic strains.

Let's say your main goal in life was to make peanut butter sandwiches. The 12 galactic strains and those being active is not going to take over, give you a new wish. But you may be surprised the recipe ideas for bread or peanuts. The different ways to grow peanuts might come through from the giants. Recipes might come through from others that now belong, in a sense, with your ancestral lineage.

The same way that you might be surprised when you learn about your biological *Homo sapiens* family history: "Oh my gosh. I didn't know I had a great grandmother who did that. I've been doing that. I've been writing poetry or singing this kind of folk song. I had no idea. I was already there. I borrowed that probably from my ancestors."

Similarly, you're going to have more tools in your toolkit and more ways of ease and fun and playfulness and certainly multidimensionality to whatever it is that you do.

Even though these are the same 12 galactic lines within you, people are not going to access them individually in the same ways, or the same frequency. Meaning, for you, you might like to draw on your dragon and giant-self quite a lot. For someone else, maybe once or twice a year. Vice versa with some of the other strains. You may ignore the reptilian largely, and someone else who is a bodybuilder or in the defensive arts might draw on that daily.

There are positive aspects to each of the 12, and neutral ones. That doesn't mean you have to use them again at any time or with any great frequency.

It's very, very important here, because this idea of free will that we had discussed at length in the first book about free will coming open for humankind—that is still very much the case. This is not a new topic in which your free will is now shut down and the galactic influences take over.

It's more like if you had been a musician who knew how to play a few different instruments. Now you know how to play a lot more, but you might still mostly play one or two of them. Maybe some of the new ones, maybe some of the old ones.

You also don't lose your old ways of being and perspective, unless you want to. So if there are things that you want to grow out of in yourself —let's say to focus on the reptilian again, for a moment—you notice that in a lot of your life, you're living from fear or that fight or flight response, like it got activated, and maybe a little overly activated, so that in in some specific instances, you feel you're over-playing that responding from fear. You can decide to grow out of that particular habit.

Similarly, in the brain space, in the mind of you, you developed some concepts and ideas of the world that must change and evolve for you to really take advantage of playing your new song with all of these new galactic notes to play—literal and figurative notes.

If you had been a horn player, your *Homo sapiens* was a horn player, and you came into all of these stringed instruments (and here we're speaking conceptually, not literally), if you have this belief system: "I only play wind instruments," Or: "I'm only a horn player, that's all I do." You do need to let go of that in order to pick up the stringed instruments and know that you can play.

Yes, there is some letting go of limitation, sense of limitation and lack. But you may still really love the horn, and that may still be the focus— the highlight. But there's just more ease and grace to that when you play. Or more stamina in your physical self that's resourced through some of these 12 lines, for example.

What you do in the world is up to you. Some of it may look to others exactly the same. But the passion, the strength, the resiliency, the perspective that you bring to it will be new. Must be new, because you have now access to so much more of yourself.

It's like saying that a twelve-year-old and a twenty-four-year-old would face the world in the same way. There's just so much growing up in the neurocircuitry and the lived life experience and the body-self between 12 years old and 24 years old. We're picking those ages a bit arbitrarily, but let's say, before you've really gone through puberty, and before your brain has finished development—we're speaking about *Homo sapiens* now. What a difference, right? You just have access to a lot more. But you still may have the leanings, the passions that you had when you were 12. But you can act on them with much greater force. And you have mental clarity in areas that weren't formed there before that could help you operationalize what you want to do in the world.

These 12 notes, strains of galactic light, allow you to operationalize what you want multidimensionally. In the concept or analogy here, the twelve-year-old may be sitting at home, doesn't really have access to the world—to drive a car, bank account or things that are needed to operationalize the vision of becoming an astronaut, let's say. The twenty-four-year-old can—enrolls in those courses, starts on that route, is out in the world becoming an astronaut.

Similarly, you may have had great desire to serve the planet, or great consciousness about the ecology of Earth or the way society is forming or dis-forming. Distortions in how society treats certain types of people, things like that. You had the heart, you had the compassion for it before. And you had the brain and the imagination to have a vision about it. But now you have, multidimensionally, resources for how to bring your vision into play, into action in this universe, this Earth.

When we speak about the 12 dimensions, again, it's not hierarchical and it's not linear. It's a wheel through you. You more or less have fifth dimension as your baseline. They are all threaded through that fifth dimensional reality, because that's where you live most of the time. Of course, you can travel especially when you're leaning into more of your giant or dragon selves. (Those are two quite interdimensional types of beings.)

Overall, the strength of you, the resilience, in terms of number of hours of energy you have in the day, will also increase. For a little while, as you're having the growing pains of these activations and what they clear out of you, you may have some waves of tiredness. But when this is complete and active in you, it is very, very awake and alive. You may find you sleep less and do more or be more—just more aliveness available to you, more attention, more alertness, more consciousness applied in your life through your different perspective lenses.

UNLIMITED MUSIC

This is Angel Raphael. As you dance your dance or sing your song of yourself in this universe, you may still like the same kind of music, but now it's played with 12 instruments instead of one. And you may discover new types of music you hadn't had the ear to listen to before —ways of viewing humankind, ideas about social structure, ideas about creative impulses you could enjoy or share with the world.

The application of these 12 and you is unlimited. The way that even though there are allegedly a limited number of notes, musical notes within the spectrum of human hearing, let's say. There are unlimited songs within that. Even though you have these 12 and there are some types of galactic beings you don't have within your DNA.

For example, Orion, you don't have that in your DNA. You might have it as a past-life memory. Your soul may have learned some things in that galaxy. But you don't come in with that in the activated New Human. But it doesn't really mean that you're limited—limited to only these 12. "Oh, no! There are other galactic beings!" Of course, and you can interact with them directly, or draw on your own memories, or learn about them.

You're not really, in that sense, limited by who your two biological parents are. Let's assume for a moment you had physical human parents, whether or not you're adopted, and that you weren't born from a petri dish. Yes, in a way, you're limited by these two parents. But not really. That's the building block. That's the musical instrument you've been given. But you can play a tremendous variety of music from those two notes. Now you have 12 more.

You don't lose what your parents, biological parents, gave you. But you do gain now what you could call your galactic forebears gave you —those 12 lines. It's additive, doesn't subtract who you are. We're spending a lot of time on this theme, even though we had discussed it in the past, because the free will element is so essential to the humans growing up here. Part of it is the activation that we've been speaking of at length, but part of it is the free will. These are additive.

DISTINCT VIBRATIONS

You may literally hear, some of you, a hum or vibration in these 12 lines that is distinct. They are each distinctly different in the way they vibrate or hum. Those of you who are visual may see different images as these different parts of yourself come online—image of a dragon or image of a giant, for example. That may be your clue that that's the energy you're working with in that hour.

For some of you, it's going to be more auditory. We're speaking about music today, also literally, because the vibration will sound distinct in these 12 lines. As we had explored in exercises in weeks prior, you can have more than one strain active that you're "playing," so to speak, playing at the same time. You can hear multiple vibrations at once as well. For some of you, it's going to be more of this auditory clue.

We would suggest not trying to map out right away with the mind. "Oh, I know that vibration, that sound. Which one is that? I need to create a flow chart." Just begin to notice, sometimes you hear a hum or a vibration, and sometimes the note or the frequency seems different. Those are different lines.

For some of you, this will be the primary way that you literally play the different dimensionalities of yourself. It's all you. But there are these different vibrational aspects that you can draw together.

Similar to a harp, you don't really often play all notes all at the same moment. Now you might play them rapid succession down the scale, and that's lovely. Or you may play a few alternating or just one for a moment. But you're not really banging on the whole harp all at once over and over again. Similarly, your body-self is not going to be that happy if you try to use all 12 perspectives, all 12 skill sets, all at once, every minute, every hour, all day long. It would sound a little bit more like noise or high school marching band on their first day of rehearsal than music.

You <u>can</u> do that, but we would suggest you and others around you are not going to enjoy that very much. But it doesn't have to be just one note at once, one vibratory field at a time.

INTERDIMENSIONAL TRAVEL VS. DIMENSIONS WITHIN YOU

If you think about this in terms of interdimensional travel, your brain gets a little overwhelmed by the idea of two lines at once. "Does that mean I'm traveling to two places at once?" We would suggest, in that sense, to think of it more like a rainbow, where the colors can bleed into one another and coexist and even form separate colors that are a blending of the two. These don't need to be side-by-side in terms of the dimensional lines but you can have more than one at one time, and that can be lovely together.

Let's speak a little bit about this distinction between interdimensional travel and living as an interdimensional being. We'll pick again on dragons and giants, because they're so easy conceptually—whether or not you believe in them—to form a mental picture and not worry too much about, right? It's a good shorthand. It is possible to travel to the dimension that giants are in, and you could do that as your *Homo sapiens* human or some other race of being. There is a place, a dimensional place, where giants reside.

There are also the giants who live there, and they are attuned to that dimensional field. But a giant can travel from where they live to third dimension, for example. The strain within you is more like the giant. It's more like the being that is attuned to the dimension of giants, than your physical body-self moving into giant dimension when you access that. It's more like accessing the giant than the dimension of giants.

Now that part of you will be so happy and awake and alive and playful were you to travel to the giant dimension, because you'd feel at home.

You'd have the right gills or eyes or arms to see and feel and touch and hold and move around if you're in the dimension of the activated line within you.

It's quite a lot for the brain to process. But we just want to touch lightly on this—that there is a distinction between you as a 12 dimensional being, traveling, let's say, to seventh dimension, and you accessing the angelic within yourself. There's a difference. Both are possible and open to you. Mostly in this topic of the 12-dimensional human, we are focused on the dimensional lines within you, not so much about traveling to other places.

The following is the transcript of a meditation. English-language audio of this meditation is available free online with the link at the end of the book.

To engage with this meditation through the words below, pause in between lines or paragraphs to listen, imagine, visualize or feel the energies described.

EXERCISE: LISTENING TO THE 12

This is Angel Ariel. We'd like to listen together to the sounds of some of the dimensional lines. We're going to ask you to focus into your heart space for this exercise, because all of the 12 lines do run through the heart.

It has to be that way because the heart is the command center. They also run through, as we had said in the past, the belly. They run through the crown. They also, all of them, run through the heart space.

You can either think of them running up and down the spine or flowing out from you in any direction. Both are accurate. Whatever is easier for your visualization right now.

We're going to ask you to focus on them one at a time, slowly at first.

What does that one dimensional line that you're focused on feel like as a vibration, or sound like to the ear? It's the same thing, but you may perceive one easier than the other.

You don't have to know which one. We're just listening to sounds, quite innocent. Like if you were playing a harp without knowing what the note names were. You just see them in space, and you're plucking one note at a time. Just for fun.

Let's try another line of the 12. Does it have a different vibration or a different sound to it?

For those of you who are quite visual, you might see this as light that pulses at different time signatures—more rapid or more slow.

Moving to the next strain. Does it have a different pulse or vibration or sound?

Moving to the next galactic line. Listening with innocence.

And the next.

And the next.

You may have some favorites. We'll give time to go back to revisit. For now, let's keep moving through to the next one.

Continue.

And another strain.

And one more here.

Rest. Just take a moment to come into silence and rest.

Some of the best music is heard or integrated best in the silence after. When you are listening to the strains of your galactic DNA, it's good to have pause moments as well.

Now if you feel you missed any of the 12, go ahead and activate those in terms of sound or vibration as you would play a note.

If you feel you have heard them all, then you could re-listen to some favorites. Or just be in stillness for a moment.

Now begin to playfully, maybe you could remember, you had a xylophone in school when you were a kid, and you just struck some of the notes with a little mallet without worrying about it being music for anyone else to hear. You were just playing. Similarly, if you'd like to return to any of these strains to just listen again or see what they're like in combination, you just play a little bit with these different vibrations, frequencies, notes, however you perceive them.

If you play them or activate them more forcefully, do they have a sharper or different note? Is it a richer tone? What happens if you play them with more force?

Or do they just get louder?

Anytime you want to, just take a rest and a break from vibration.

21

WHY TWELVE?

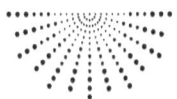

In reference to the Listening to the 12 Exercise from the previous chapter. **Some of these sounds like wind gusts, like bumpy vibration. Another one felt like a vision in my eyes. The energy was in my eyes. Another one air. How is air sound?**

I wonder if the angels could help us a little bit with, should we just not bother interpreting it and just keep going like that?

This is Raphael. Yes, the less you interpret the best, because what you're looking for is to form patterns. If it's just a one-off: "Okay, well, there's just interesting sensations and lights. I don't know what to make of this." Better to just let the mind relax. "That's okay, mind. Maybe it was nothing." But then the seventh time that you see the same purple flash, you think: "Huh. All right, there's a consistency to this." And maybe you start to map it, in a sense.

We don't mean map like geography, but was that the dragon purple? Then you start to get curious. And then you do form a mental knowing. But it's through repetition, through patterns, that emerge and evolve.

189

The initial spectrum of experience, we would say, the less you interpret, it helps you the most. Because your mind in this life right now has mostly been trained to third-dimensional knowing. You're opening up into very different frequencies of being, and the mind will be kind of the last to get on board. The happier or more relaxed you can be with those times when you don't know how to interpret, the easier it is for you to integrate all of this into your way of life.

You will have come to that moment where you understand what's going on. But that's not the first step for most of you. Because the mind is, again, very attuned to very specific ways of seeing and knowing, essentially third-dimensional.

Obviously, there's a reason that they give us this exercise. Is the intention to practice this exercise more so to enrich our experience?

This is Raphael. Yes. It's very similar to when you're learning piano and you have exercises. The scales themselves or the little nursery rhyme song themselves are not very important, but it teaches you to stretch your fingers in a certain way. Or just to explore. Or to hear different notes over and over until you can recognize major and minor keys, those kind of things.

Not everyone is auditory, so we force a little bit: "Well, just listen anyway." And not everyone is visual, but we force a little bit those exercises. "Well just look around anyway. Maybe you won't see anything." But these are exercises, right? The point is to stretch a bit from where you are now, and just in innocence, observe.

A question about the notion of playing consciously versus having things come to us. Adria has shared the story about the interactions with the giant in a couple of instances, which I think she probably hadn't called in consciously. We know that we have these strands available, and so we can play with them. What's a beautiful way to play consciously, or just allowing these influences to come to us in a way that's maybe not so deliberately called in?

This is Angel Raphael. When you have a guide that is external to yourself, in this case, Adria has a giant guide, right? Not all of you do. Not because she is more special. She just signed up to have a giant guide, and the giant guide signed up to have her. When you have a guide that is external to yourself, and many people rely on Pleiadian and another galactic guides, whether they are through channels or personal guides. That is a literal being that is outside of yourself.

Now, when you have a galactic strain of Pleiadian or giant, that is the DNA of that species. It has the abilities and the perception and the notes, if you like, of that species. You're not looking to make contact with an individual being when you are playing these notes or reflecting on some activated part of yourself. It's not going to show up like a guide on the outside of yourself. Now, you may have images of beings that come with that collective memory. The same way that you have images if you think back on your childhood. There are images there of people in them. That doesn't mean that there is a person external to yourself when you're calling up that memory.

And then dragons have different ways of seeing, so the light will look different, and so on, through them. And through you when that is active in you. That's very different than sitting in your yard and having a conversation with a dragon.

Now, you may do both. But what's active in you is not an external being. It is the potential that dragons or giants carry within them—ways of seeing, ways of in a multidimensional sense calling in resources, or influencing light and sound, some of these dimensional capabilities like that—that you'll come into with greater and greater ease and understanding as you play with them, practice. The same way that young children instinctually know how to walk. They might take some practice and how to dance. But what type of dance? How fast or slowly you walk, and then skipping and all of that comes later. But doesn't really take very long.

First you may just be stumbling around a little. Really, we like this term play. Not just because it's lighthearted. But because it assumes that you're not trying to fit into a tight box or get something right. You're just messing around to see: "How does this work? What is this perception? What is the skill? What does it look like? What does it taste like? What does it feel like?" Just to play. Then you can do serious things with it or not. It's up to you. Again, you can stay making peanut butter sandwiches.

Okay, I'm in a situation, and it would might be helpful to have some other perspectives. Which of the 12 might have something to suggest?

This is Raphael. Sometimes you'll know instinctually. "I think I want to ask my Lyran DNA about this. Get an informed perspective." And sometimes you might want to methodically go through all 12, once you know what they all are. Both are correct. It's fine.

You're not going to then have to walk through life so slowly, because at every vantage point and every choice point, you have to stop and consult all 12. But it's a good starting place when you're stuck, or when you feel: "I have some extra time and I'm a little bored. What do any of the 12 have to say?"

You could just play that way. So that it's more real time. What's meaningful to you in the moment? Which might be just: "What does this flower look like through the vantage point of all the 12?" and seeing how light and perception of light is differs.

You can be very playful and very practical. And certainly if you get in a sticky situation, whether it's mental or emotional or physical: "I wonder if I have new resources for this now? And I don't have to just tough it out or wait for help from the outside. I wonder if there's some help or perspective or physicality from the inside that could help me now."

Some of you might, if you chose to, now become stonemasons, because you have this giant activated in you, for example. There are creative aspects that you have the ability to draw on as well—artisan creative aspects.

This is Raphael. Lyran and Sirian are there as well. We have touched on those very briefly. Andromedan as well. Those are some of the more familiar galactic types of beings. We won't spend very long on each of them. We started on purpose with types of creatures that you could relate to very easily because you've seen them in a children's story or read about them in some fantasy novel, or seen them in your own visions. Many cultures have art depictions of angels and dragons and so on. We started with some that, even if it's wrong, the mind could easily call up an image or have an idea: "Oh, a giant. I know what a giant is. It's a very big person. Okay."

Because if we say Pleiadian or Sirian, sometimes, if we'd started with that with the early exercises, people are wondering: "Are they blue? Are they green? I forgot. Am I supposed to know what this being is?"

We really won't be detailing every aspect of all of the 12. We will tell you what they all are by the end of going through these topics. But we do want you to more innocently from your own perspective experience what that is.

Because there is misinformation out there, or there's old information —how one or three dragons behaved 505,000 years ago is not necessarily all that you have access to. It may be factually very accurate, but it may be limited.

We do want you to feel very empowered to have your own experience of what these 12 galactic strains mean. Even if you were to travel to a spaceship to meet an external being who is a Sirian. They would tell you all about themselves. Well, that's one Sirian. You have access to the whole genetic line, through you.

We don't want you to get so defined in your vision of what you think these 12 are that you miss some of the more wonderful or creative aspects that maybe weren't talked about in a certain novel or from a certain guide's vantage point. We will speak a little bit at least about all of the 12, but we started with the ones that are more obvious.

Because again, even if you have misconceptions of giants or dragons or angels, you know what that is. So your mind relaxes and says: "Oh, sure, sure. I got that." That's why we've spent more time on those. Not because they're more important or more popular. It's just easier.

When we're going through activations and exercises, the more innocent you are in the brain space of what's really happening, the more you can really take in the wonder and the awe and the newness and what really is there. Because no *Homo sapiens* mind really has had access to these 12 galactic lines with such purity and strength before.

So your mind, even if it was to read an encyclopedia about each, can't really help you get there. But the activation and the beingness of it— you already are there. The same way that you could have read a lot about humans before you were born. But living three years on Earth, you sure grew a lot and understood, in a very visceral way, what it is to be human. Much, much more than reading about it will tell you.

On purpose, we're not going to instruct you what these are. "Here's the good and the bad of them." Or: "Here are the three things you can do as a dragon." But we'll point out some examples so you don't feel totally lost in conceptual reality.

But from there, please, trust what you do know and feel, even if you never read a story that said a dragon had different kind of eyesight and was so passionate about color. But you might have noticed that there are a lot of colorful gemstones and colorful dragons in a lot of these stories. So part of it was picked up on, just maybe not the whole of it.

I *was surprised when reptilian was mentioned, because it seems like what I've heard of that strain or has been more in the negative.*

This is Raphael. Yes, reptilian is one of the 12, and they represent some beautiful strengths in terms of your mammal self, let's say. They also are highly intelligent. We're not saying they are dumb animals. But we would say that when you are accessing the reptilian in yourself, because all of them are choice points now, it most often is going to be around that physical strength—the hardened shell of you. If you think of reptilian skin versus human skin. When you need that tough shell, or when you need that fight in you—might only be 12 or three or one time you need that in your life, but you have access to a stronger version of that than perhaps your *Homo sapiens* self knows about.

There are strengths to that. And if you were to be limited to that, if you were to move from *Homo sapiens* to pure reptilian, perhaps you would feel that was too hard of a transition, and not when you would choose. However, we would suggest it is a strength to have it as one of the twelve.

Much of this will be practical or fun. In other words, not life or death and not saving the world. Yet, when you practice with all of these fun things, you get so much closer to what we would call unification and peace. Peaceful understanding of different races. It can have very practical ramifications in terms of galactic war or lack of war. And in terms of subsistence life on Earth. Many, many widespread applications here for humankind.

Even if you start very playfully in your own daily life, and no one's going to live or die or feel that they had a mystical journey because of where you planted a potted plant into the Earth, something in you has changed. Little by little, you're going to find you have so many different ways of perceiving and receiving information and influencing the world around yourself.

By influence we mean sound and light and frequency vibration, thought, conscious intent, things like that. So many nuances of that. Understanding, perceiving the world and also influencing the world around you.

PHILOSOPHY AND INTENT

When almost everyone can access these 12 strains, will people be in a higher dimension in consciousness at that time? For instance, reptilian, could this be used in a real negative way to do harm?

It's a beautiful question. This is Raphael. We'll speak a little bit now about philosophy or intent. Why choose more than one galactic strain when forming humankind?

Galactic beings, as you know or may imagine, have their own version of warfare and mystical journeys and things that are important to them that they would want to enhance or replicate or change. In the creation of humankind with these 12 galactic strands, the idea was to find a balance. Exactly to address that question you had of: "What if we created a being that was so strong and then they were too powerful and they did damage to all of us (the founding galactic beings)?"

The idea is, you have a harmony of 12. Of course, these are not the only galactic races, and they're not the most important or the highest, necessarily. They are just the 12 that wanted to come together for this formation of humankind. The parents, if you like, of humankind.

196

When you have all of those 12 active in you, and one of them does have tendency towards violence, for example, or tendency towards quietness, but it's only one of the 12, you then have balance points. You have other choice points. It's a little bit like having a democracy of 12 instead of a dictatorship of one.

In the case of reptilian, the other dimensional aspects of you most often are going to be higher vibratory frequency understanding of the situation, and are going to outweigh that mammalian or hierarchical response in most cases. And in some cases, that will be the very best, most compassionate, kindest, most direct way to proceed, the reptilian way. Even when you're speaking about compassion and uplift, there is a balance. Or philosophically speaking, the idea behind combining these 12.

It's not like combining parents in the sense of you'll get one eye color and one ear shape, but combining meaning, you get everything. Access to all of the eye colors in an interior sense. That analogy is false, but just to give you an idea. It's not about mix and match, and you got some of them and someone else got some of the other traits. You have all of them.

When you have all of them, there's more of a sense of understanding: "This is not the only perspective. I have 12 just within me. And there must be at least 20, 40, 100 other types of galactic beings. My goodness, what a wide world this is! I can see value to a lot of these different perspectives, even though they're contradictory or they don't have the same approach or the same skills to approach with."

Unification and peace is the philosophical intent behind combining the 12, for exactly that reason. Not to create a monster, but to create a highly intelligent, highly powerful being. What you do with that? Again, even highly intelligent, highly powerful beings can play, can create, can do other things than what is "important," or life-saving, or world saving. And you have more access to those things too. All of that is true.

And because it's not just you, they didn't create just one New Human, here are many, many, many, many, many of you, you also don't fall into that false trap of: "Ah, I'm the powerful one. I'm going to dominate everyone else who is weak." Instead, it is this shared symphony of power and empowerment, joy and enjoyment. "Here we are, and we are so multidimensional." It becomes more difficult to draw a hard line in terms of politics or war. Because even within yourself, you can become aware there's a lot more than one perspective, and so you stop fighting for the one right way.

We would say, from angelic perspective, there is a wisdom and a truth, most likely a truth to the fact that this will result in more peace than war.

And the humans that are ready for this? Are there two paths, the high road and the low road kind of thing, frequency wise, or consciousness level?

Absolutely. This is Raphael. Not higher and lower in terms of judgment, good and bad or lesser and better. But higher and lower in terms of frequency, absolutely. There are those who will choose to remain dormant in these aspects. Each and every human has these 12 lines within them. It's not a special gift for the special few. Everyone has them. And there is a free will choice point, so that each human alive now can decide: "Do I want to activate this now while I'm on Earth?"

There will be, of course, more than two kinds of people or two kinds of circumstance. But essentially, there is a vibrational divide between those who are staying more or less third-dimensional and dormant in these aspects, and those who are choosing to activate these 12 lines and live a much more multidimensional life expression.

From an angelic perspective, one of these choices is not better than the others. You could just trust each person's individual wisdom (whether it's unconscious or conscious), whether or not it's for them to activate that in this life. What's important from the angelic perspective is that it's available for everyone to access.

We see these two as complementary and coexisting. If you think about below the water (ocean, a river), and then above in the air, there's different kinds of creatures. And there's no problem. Earth doesn't have to have one or the other, it has both. Similarly coexisting, you'll find people who are living out more traditional third-dimensional linear type stories and feeling more limited in themselves, _feeling_, not that they are limited. And then those who are choosing to activate.

It might be more like 1/3 or maybe up to 1/2 of the population. Not that there's a limit, but that's what we see right now, in terms of numbers of people who might choose this. It will always remain open. Those who get wind of the idea through a relative or a friend or a podcast and say: "Oh, I want that. Okay, great, you can have it. It's not one timepoint choice point. It's really open now to anyone at any time.

These are complementary, in our view, they will coexist for a while. The third-dimensional way will eventually phase out. New babies coming in will be already alert with the twelve.

22
MULTI-DIMENSIONAL IN PRACTICAL EVERYDAY USE

This is Angel Raphael. Essentially, energy is more. When you had one source which was *Homo sapiens*, although there were different mixes of genetics in that, then you move to 12 sources, a collective DNA, the purity of collective DNA of 12 galactic races, what you have is more energy.

Because some groups take focus and energy from light. Some focus and energy from different types of food or social interaction or collective atmosphere, in other words, the hum, or the hub of social will. Not quite exactly the same with any of these, but the way that bees gather energy from themselves, from the hive.

Similarly, some of these galactic races, and we'll speak about more of them today, have a buzz that they get from other beings. So you have more energy, more resources at your disposal. And you can use that for daily life or big projects, for the big vision, whatever it is. And all of the above. Just like in your *Homo sapiens* life, you use the energy, the fuel that you have, for many, many different things.

The short CliffsNotes version of today's topic is you'll have more. More energy for everything. And when you have more energy, you tend to do more as well—take on new projects, or feel you can take that vacation or give more to others, because you don't feel in a sense of lack or deprivation yourself. It does affect many, many waves of how you function in the world.

Even if it were the same kind of energy, which it is not, just turning up the volume of energy means you have more. Similar to how people used to feel so tied to the monetary aspects—if they have more money, they could do more. Similarly, we would say energy is more of the primary resource in this new era. When you have more of it, you have more capacity for whatever you choose. Free will is still quite important. So what you choose is up to you.

At the same time, it's not the same energy, it's not the same frequency of light that you are used to. And it's not just one new frequency, it is 12.

This means you have a multidimensionality to the way you view the world and the way you function in it, in very practical and deep mystical ways. There's nothing that's left out of this transformation. In other words, it's not just for the mystic aspects of your life, and it's not just for the practical ones. It is for both.

Because some of these twelve will bring into your awareness things you have never thought to be conscious of before, such as perhaps the buzz, the social buzz we were speaking of, which isn't exactly parties so much as collective will towards social change and betterment—group projects, that kind of thing on a massive scale. You may just never have been involved in that, or may not have occurred to you to be involved in that. And suddenly, the inspiration and the opportunity and the energy for that is there. This may change your life in practically profound ways as well.

A FEW MORE OF THE 12

Let's speak a little bit more about the 12. Then we'll move into some other related topics here about your energy field.

Pleiadian we had touched on briefly—overview and diplomacy, some had shared that perspective when they tune into their own Pleiadian nature. Because this society, over time, over many generations, was involved in great galactic warfare, they have come now to be more the peace-mongers. Those that generate peace, talk about peace, and speak about the diplomatic channels, ways of achieving that—through the practical experience of what is the opposite, those many decades and more of war. That society has evolved. In you, you have the highest evolution of that.

Sirian are highly technical, and you have your choice of what you use that technical capacity for and with. Sirians do tend to be individualistic, more so than some of the other 12. This might be that great invention you feel you want to take credit for. Some technological insight or invention. Space travel, technology-assisted health, those are two of the areas here that are quite similar in nature and that it leans on technology applied in different new ways. Those are natural elements for Sirian, the Sirian in you.

There's a healing intelligence, you might call it quantum field—which could be for healing, but also can be with shifting reality. From human perspective, it looks highly scientific in nature. Where some of the other beings might be perceived more compassionately.

In other words, you feel their love or their heart or their friendship more from a sense of warmth, or what you might interpret as an emotional point of view, caring point of view. Sirian may appear to be cold, calculating, intellectual, but really it's just that they are highly attuned to the intellect and to quantum fields. It does come from a very beneficent place, but it might not appear to you so much as: "Oh, this is my friend" as "this is someone who came in to assist."

Or, like the engineer who comes in to build the planet. They are world builders as well. Your Earth is an organic world, but many are not. From human perspective, highly technical in nature. Quantum might be a better word there.

Lyran we have touched on briefly. Musics, all kinds of music come from Lyran. We don't mean to say that every music on Earth now is Lyran in nature. But that the Lyran in you contains all types of music. Music and musicality—appreciation of music, generation of music, musical collaboration, different types of instrumentation you might not have thought of before. Music in the wind and rain. The ability to perceive music in all things is a very Lyran trait.

This is not one planet. There's a constellation there. Vega, the star system Vega. Some of you know this word vegan. These are beings that are very attuned to the cosmology of insects and animal-kind and why they have their own wisdom and brilliance. If there's a part in you that lights up around this zoology, cosmology of conscious life— insect, mammal and so on—it may be this knowledge from this planet Vega. This is within the Lyran strand here of the DNA.

Arcturians, on the quantum level and the physical, are highly technological. Quantum, scientific knowledge and deep understanding of how things work on the practical physical level, or not so practical. Many have spoken about "med beds," and of course, that could come from elsewhere as well, but Arcturians absolutely have that capability to do advanced healing very rapidly. Technology used for good or science curiosity. We would say those are two of the hallmarks. Physically, they are blue beings, similar, not quite the same, as human. You wouldn't mistake an Arcturian for a human wearing blue paint, but two arms, two legs, a little more recognizable.

When you think of galactic or starseed, you think of more of these races more typically. Yes, you have some of those as well. But not everyone relates yet to those. We saved those until toward the end to discuss some of that.

Whether or not you ever had a lifetime there, you're opening up to these capacities within yourself. In moving back or forward, so any of your concurrent lives, you also have the option as a soul to live out time on any of those planetary systems. They're all still awake and alive, have not been destroyed.

As you become friendly or familiar with those aspects within yourself, some of that may inform your next lifetimes. It's not necessarily that they're familiar to you from the so called "past." Maybe you'll jump into some of them in the future when you're done with Earth, or want to take a pause from Earth and visit somewhere else for a lifetime.

Interplanetary travel in this life is absolutely available. But we'll mostly speak in this transmission about what it means to be on Earth with these activated. Because not everyone's going to be interested in traveling elsewhere. This is more about the New Human on Earth as it is now, which is also a New Earth, or new bandwidths of frequency of Earth.

ONE-WAY STREET

Old Earth begins to fade more and more from view, from consciousness. It is still available galactically, and for those on Earth. Old Earth is still available as a choice point.

You never have to feel rushed or forced into all of this newness of you. However, it is a bit of a one-way street. Now you can walk, or crawl, or occasionally hopscotch, or jump a foot or two on a one-way street. You don't have to travel quickly. But you don't really go back to the old you, the way the butterfly doesn't shove back into a caterpillar. Just wouldn't make sense.

It's an evolution of you into more. And so you don't go back to less. But you remember where you came from. So you can still relate with those on Old Earth, or have memories of your life in this life as *Homo sapiens.*

But you do become something else. The evolution out of *Homo sapiens* to what we're calling New Human. We'll leave the naming of what that is to someone else.

POWER

The X-Men character who has come to life has gone through some transformation. And either is always that way or has a bit of a back-and-forth switch, like Wolverine. They don't really go back to how they lived before. But they remember. They might have friends or pastimes or relatives from their old life.

But you don't really go back to believing you are powerless. In this case, the powers that you are empowering in you are not so much about war and warfare as those comics have highlighted (at least through recent authors). This idea that it's about a battle all of the time, and that's what strength is for.

To angelic viewpoint, the strength in the New Human is not very much about battle. That's not what you're preparing for here. That's not the practical application of all these empowerments. That's important, because in your own mind and in our analogies, we have pointed to comic book hero type of transformations. And usually in those comic book stories, there's a battle with a nemesis or a government, or some other beings from other planets, or something like that. That's not what we see for humankind.

You have all this power and empowerment. Yes, it does make you stronger, but it also doesn't mean that you're headed for battle. "So gosh, what does that mean then? What if I am this new, empowered creation, and it's not about warfare? Wow. What would I use all of that power for?"

That's where you get to use your imagination to wonder: "Huh, if daily life didn't have to be about just getting by, and if daily life was also not about some big war or battle, what could daily life be about?"

That's where some of you jump into the big societal thinking, or exploratory thinking—exploring new worlds, new planets. Or improving the one that you're on. Or relaxing into the change between feeling oppressed and oppression to empowered and powerful.

Each of you still have your perspective of how you live life. Some of you are very internal in how you process and relate to life. Deeply introspective would be one way of being internal. Some of you are very external, maybe social, or more on display in how you live your life. That still applies. We don't see that changing. Although as you become more aware of all your different skill sets here, you might shift in some of those ways as well. But just start with what's comfortable and natural to you.

Because, again, you're not being asked to use all 12 actively all of the time. But it's very good to begin to practice, learning about, looking at, feeling into: "What is the wisdom that comes from my Pleiadian self?" Or: "What is the embodied expression of my Pleiadian self? What does it feel like to walk around a room feeling this way?"

That's the exercise we're going to do today. You might some of you need to do this later if someone else is in the room or something like that. It's a simple exercise. You can always just read about it and apply it later on.

EMBODIMENT EXERCISE

As you read, you can pause in between each set of instructions to move around. Then come back to read the next part when you feel ready.

Essentially, we're going to play with walking around in these different embodied energies. It's not going to look like modern dance adaptation, where you're in an ape, gorilla, you know, and then a

207

flying being. You don't have to be silly or dramatic about it, but you also don't have to hold back. It's okay to be playful.

But sometimes it feels subtle. Yet the more that you practice and play with: "What does my embodied self feel about this?" In other words, you're an energy body. You're a soul. You also have feet and legs and nose and toes. That's what we mean by embodied. What does the body feel about these 12? is the practical aspect we're going to explore together today.

If you are able where you are now, give yourself a little room to move around. Doesn't have to be a vast space.

Just take a few breaths first to feel your body in the room, in space. That might be what the bottoms of your feet feel like on the floor or in your socks, your stockinged feet. Or what your nose feels like, the outside of your nose hitting the air in the room. Any part of your physical self, just what it feels like right now—whether it's discomfort or neutral. Feeling the definition of your physical self. This has been given to you essentially as your vehicle for your energies and your thoughts and your wishes and your prayers to live out in this life.

And it does adjust according to your wish. The simplest way of describing this is when you want to rest and sleep, the body behaves very differently than when you want to go run a marathon. It's responding to your requests.

As you walk around or move gently, lightly around your room, why don't you choose one of these 12 that you're aware of—you could say Sirian, for example—and ask for your body to feel what that part of your new DNA feels like in you. Again, it may not be dramatic. But is there anything you notice as you move your physical self? What does Sirian feel like?

This is not a Sirian walk-in. This is your galactic DNA—comes from the planet Sirius.

What does it physically, viscerally, feel like in you? Does it change the way your toes and heels hit the floor when you walk around? Does it feel heavier in places that are different than when you walk around as your everyday self?

If you want to come back to neutral, sitting or standing, and just breathe where you are for a moment. Feeling the contrast to yourself as you usually define it, and the Sirian embodiment. It may just be a few aspects that feel different, and most feels the same. That's what we would expect, that there's a little bit of an uncommon heaviness in one part of the body, or more of a focus towards hearing or seeing or smelling than usual, that kind of thing.

Now let's switch to Pleiadian, asking that strain of galactic Pleiadian DNA to embody in you in such a way that you can feel what parts of your physical self might activate differently, as you walk around, move around your room.

When you're ready, come back. Let's do a third one here.

Coming back again to the contrast, and here you can hold the three: your let's call it original self and Sirian and Pleiadian all at once. Feeling the distinction. We're just contrasting Pleiadian with original self. Always good to feel the contrast. Sometimes new insights will come up from that. Then moving into the third one for today, which is dragon. Just being innocent. No one's watching. So you can be dramatic or fanciful if you want. And it may be more subtle than you think.

Again walking or moving around your room as dragon. How does that galactic DNA of dragon race inform how you move in this human self? It's not going to shape-shift you into a physical dragon someone else could see. But it does activate different parts of you. How does that embody as you move around your room?

Is there any other aspect of dragon that you hadn't noticed yet? As you move around, enamored of what this might open up for you in your physical self.

Again, contrasting now, yourself, human self, with the dragon part of your human self and any of the others that you walked with today.

Coming back when you feel ready to your however you usually sit or stand when reading the transmission here.

HISTORY AND PRESENCE

This is Raphael. There's a reason why we're not going into the galactic histories of these different races, or long lists of: here's what it looks like. Here's what the physical capabilities are, or the mental view. Because anything we could tell you along those lines is going to be factual and historical.

When you were looking at Sirian, a Sirian being that is 100% genetically Sirian, that has to be different than a being that is 1/12th Sirian, right? There is an alchemy to the combination of these 12 in you that is yours to admire and explore and create. It's new. So we can't tell you, really.

We do give a few pointers that feel true about how these embody or how these play out in the New Human. But please understand that it is genetics in you. It's not a race history or what Sirians have done in the past to or with other races, for example. Doesn't matter, really.

What does the Sirian in you activate and make possible? Then from there, what do you want to act out or act upon? Because, just because you have the ability to be a marathon runner doesn't mean you have to run a marathon. Or that you have to run more than one, if you get inclined and you feel like you don't like it so much.

There is a purity to the genetic strains. Meaning, it's not about the soul history, it's about the full potential of that race. It also is in combination. That's one of the reasons why we're not giving you long lists of "this is what to expect will activate in you from this race line."

The combination, the alchemy, and also your free will in which parts of these to really utilize, not just have active and available, but really utilize. Each of you are going to walk a distinct different path with this. And it may change over time.

If any of these, let's say the reptilian, in you feel: "Oh no. I've heard all of these terrible things about history." Okay, maybe some of those are true. But what is the reptilian in you going to do in this life?

What are the access points to different ways of being and different ways of thinking? Becoming familiar with it as it is in you gives you the most power to either act upon or refrain from acting on. Again, it's not out of balance. You're not 11/12ths reptilian and 1/12th dragon. You have quite a lot to choose from.

That was on purpose as well, to have quite a lot of races genetically giving input to create a wider, more powerful, more well-balanced— balanced in terms of perspective, and balanced in terms of ability—a more balanced you.

Energy is one of the ways in which you are better resourced now. Physical embodiment of different characteristics is going to become quite important. Again, here's where the analogy to the comic book hero or visuals you might have of dragons or reptilians or Pleiadians may not serve you as well. Because physically you're going to look more or less the same as you are now.

Others who are going through this transformation might be able to perceive something in your eyes, or the way the energy glows off your body, things like that. That might give them a clue. "Oh, this being has more going on than they did when they were 12. There's something else active in them." It is recognizable to some degree, but not in the comic book hero sense, where the very physical, visceral transition more like shape-shifting takes place. That's not what we're going on about here.

At the same time, it is very real in you. This is not a fictional character in some future Earth. This is now in you in in this life. The transformation will not be, as we said, overnight. That's out of compassion for you to ramp up to holding this much energy and this much different types of potential kinetics. Kinetics is mostly what we were exploring today.

The body is also in time and space, more or less. Different aspects of these 12 have different relationships to time and space. That is the other sensory experience, which we can't point to as easily with walking around the room.

One of your senses in *Homo sapiens* is: where are you physically in space and time? You have different ways of perceiving space and time through these 12. Angelic, as we mentioned, is not in time in the same way. When you want to step out of the confines of time, you could lean a little more on your angelic self, for example. Some of these galactic beings are very, very good at manipulating space—phasing in and out of different places, and that kind of thing.

You will have access to different ways of being in time and space through these 12 as well. That's part of the embodied experience, as it activates in you, as you become experimental and more aware and alive in yourself. It's just through trial and error. You're not going to get it wrong.

Some things may occur to you in dreams. You might have a different color palette or a different food craving, different way of movement on the dance floor. Things that don't alarm anyone else, but you notice: "Oh, wow, that's different. I didn't used to like the color orange at all." Playful, playful, exotic, let's say, different ways of living life.

23

THE CLEAR AND PLACID LAKE

This is Angel Raphael. You are doing, engaging in, so much activation, and here on 12 fronts. We have spoken of you as the hub through the heart or the belly, umbilical cord, spinal column. It's more than one transit area. It's very networked in. But essentially you are the hub.

You conceive of yourself as a very active center, consciously wishing, shaping these perceptions and gifts into how you want to navigate your world. And it's important to have a rest point. Because you don't really have "you" any longer as you go through these transformations.

Your soul is still there. Your brain still remembers the life story more or less. Your body still looks more or less the same from the outside. The exterior of you is still there. People can still see you walking through space and time around your neighborhood. In your life, the cast of characters are largely still there. But you don't really have yourself in the same way to rely on—the you, let's say *Homo sapiens* you, that you grew up with.

That *Homo sapiens* you had found resting points, benchmarks, places to hold on to when weather got rough or things just got too much.

213

You had places within yourself where you knew how to center, redirect, calm and so on.

What we're going to do together is find that new place in you. There will be more than one, but we're going to create one today together, so that you have a resting place in in storms of high energy, yes, but more importantly, the energy is you. Now you're going to have so many energies running through your system in different ways, you want to have the capacity to be able to turn that down.

You don't really shut yourself off. The way you never really did before, but you could meditate or sleep, walk in nature around a placid lake and find these places of rest. Similarly, the new you wants places of rest, repose.

We use this image of a calm and placid lake as a metaphor. It's not literal. But for many of you, that is a very calming influence, especially in the heat of summer. Some of you are in part of the world where it's quite hot right now or dry. The water is also nourishing, but it's a calm nourishment.

It's not a flood, it's not a waterfall. There's a calmness and a depth to it. A lake is not going to run out. So you don't have to fear: "I don't have very much time in this calm space." Or: "Not very much water to drink". It's this deep, nourishing, restful place.

We're going to create that with you, so that you have at least one anchor point in your now self that is reliably calm and secure. We use the word secure, not to say that the rest of you is insecure or unsafe, but it's very fluid. The world is chaotic and fluid now.

You as a dimensionally shifting being, are much more fluid. Your abilities are fluid. Your life is going to have more rapid change and interplay now. Because it's a different way of being. You're going to work through things, play through things, receive things much more quickly. The life story also seems like it's sped up, somehow. It's not just because you're older, and that saying that "time flies" as you age. Because of the fluidity and how fast you can get your wishes now.

If you can get a house in a month or an hour instead of 10 years or 30 years, well, then what do you wish for next? Even if it's all positive, or largely so, it's still moving through quite quickly. It's nice to have those places of stillness, essentially out of time and out of activity. Even though we use water here as a metaphor, the lake itself is a place out of time and out of activity. That's why it's a placid lake. Not because it is stagnant, but because it moves, oscillates; it's alive. But it is also still, quite still and placid.

We will be doing a meditative exercise together now. If you'd like to, sit in your chair or get comfortable how you are when you meditate or rest, and reflect with us.

∿

English-language audio of this meditation is available free online with the link at the end of the book.

Adria: If you prefer to read this meditation. I suggest feeling or imagining the energies as you read about them, and then close your eyes to rest in that energy.

MEDITATION: A PLACE OF REST

This is Angel Raphael. Becoming aware, first, of energy moving both up and down through the spine. Above you and below you and all the way through the spine, there is a clear white light. It looks transparent to some of you. It looks white to others. It's the same thing to the angelic.

A clear white light up and down through the spinal column. Feel the energy and activation of that. That's going to energize any places in you that feel lackluster right now because of so much change.

Now we're going to ask you to create in your heart field—that might be wider than the organ of the heart. It might be about shoulder to shoulder, or it might extend out from your body.

Essentially a horizontal field at about the level of the heart as big as feels natural. This is not a time for efforting and forcing "bigger is better." No, whatever size and shape came up automatically, that's about right. It may be different on different days. Smaller is fine. It's just a horizontal plane. It's very still. It oscillates it's alive, but it's very serene, still. About the level of the heart on a horizontal plane.

Now this area is beyond time. If you're feeling rushed or like things are moving too slow in what do you want to happen, you can come to this place to have a rest from that pressure of time. If you're feeling "I'm not enough" or "the world isn't giving me what I want," this is a good place to come to rest, to be out of time.

You're just breathing and noticing this place in you. For some of you, it may feel in a tactile sense, that it's there, ready for you. For others, you might see gently a horizontal, placid field. It may feel fluid, or it may feel still. But it shouldn't feel like a structure, like something like a block. It's soft.

This is your resting place. Not a place of stagnation, but a place of deep rest. You are creating this within yourself. So it exists; it resides in you for all time. Or as long as you want it to. If for any reason you decide you don't want this anymore, you can just dissolve it. Today, let's focus on creating this so that you can return whenever you like to this sense of placid and still, outside of the pressures of time.

Some dimensions are in time the way you have known it. Some are not. Having a reference point that is outside of time is also helpful. There's a reason why we placed it in the center that's also the command center. You'll see this overlap and interchange as you get more nuanced with yourself in these other dimensions.

For now just have it as a standalone—placid waters, still waters, of a restful place outside of time, in you.

Your mind doesn't have to create this. It's just your intent. Then whatever visual sense or felt sense arises to match that. Could even be an emotional sense. Some of you feel it better that way.

There's nothing to do in this space. Nothing to decide. Nothing to get done. No pressures of time. You're not late or slow, and you're not early in this place.

Very gently ,when you're ready, gently come out of this place to what you know as your room. Allow that sense of the placid and still to maintain, to stay with you. It's an overlap of sorts.

What you have created is literally a place within yourself, although it is not in time, it is a place. It's not an imagination or "I'll just calm down now," sort of attitude. It's a place.

You have the reference point now you can either just find it within yourself, or re-read or re-listen when you want to come out of time and be in a place of quiet.

Some of you may eventually hear music there. By quiet we mean not the rush, not the busy, not the "I'm late. I have things to do."

Complete rest.

～

I f I go there, to the place of rest, am I opting out of benefiting from energies coming in—the good energies? And secondly, if I go there, if it's a day that I do want to function actively out in the world, I presume that's not the day to go to the place of rest?

This is Raphael. Beautiful vantage point here. For the first part: Can I take in new energies while in rest? Yes, you may. We don't think we need to go into technologically why that is the case. But yes, you may. Similarly, can you then go from rest to activity? Well, if you think of how much more able you are to be active after a good, deep rest, like a good night's sleep versus fitful sleep or no sleep, then yes, it's the same thing.

You come back from the place of rest, restored, recharged and ready to act. Or, ready to be and just observe and witness, but from a sense that's more buoyed, not so torn down or worn down by the mental alert or the emotional clearing kind of frictious energies. Yes, you can always experiment and play, and if it really calms you down too much, you say: Well, maybe I better do this just in the evenings for a while."

But we would imagine that if you're feeling the stress point enough to want to visit this place during the day, you probably need it to have that balance and center to then be able to act from a calmer place, which is more efficient with activity. You'll just have to experiment and know yourself. Does it make you too spacey to drive, or something like that? Then you maybe just visit at night.

M*aybe a good way to look at it is like it's a place of meditation or a quiet, like you take an hour out to do it.*

Absolutely yes. Similar to meditation. Once you find that place over and over again, and the reference point becomes easier to slot into, you can do this for five minutes or an hour or overnight. You can just play with that. But it becomes easier as a quick reference point.

Some people count to 10 or take three or 10 breaths. Like that, you may be able to do it on the go. Not necessarily while your eyes are open operating a crane or a power tool, but more or less on the go, during life. It can become a "quick fix" tool as well. Or take a longer time in the deep rest.

24

DESIGNED TO ASCEND

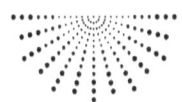

When we activate these 12 galactic strands, how does it impact these galactic races? If there's something like quantum entanglement, if something awakens in us, what does it do to them?

This is Angel Raphael. Not so much as you might think. In other words, if you think of someone being asleep versus awake, an asleep human is still doing quite a lot in their inner spaces on the quantum level. Similarly, this has been dormant in you. The galactic strains have been dormant within you. The fact that you're waking up to them, that in and of itself doesn't have a direct quantum impact. Because what's activating is not something new—the individual strains.

Let's say there's the Lyran strain. It gets activated. The Lyrans are not going to learn something from that, because it's already in their DNA. Other galactic beings have already experienced what Lyran energy feels like.

However, when you start to live from a quantum place of these 12 activations informing your skill set, your perception and so on, that's where the quantum news hits the universe, in terms of change or potential for new awarenesses to spread like that.

Most of you are not quite there yet, where you're really living from these places of "this is the dragon part of me in my daily life. And how does it mix with the Lyran? What new information or knowledge or perception does that create?

That will begin to happen more and more in the coming year, with each of you who are taking this in, and becoming active. Then, yes, it becomes quantum news in the universe, where change occurs just by you being that. But just waking up to what you are, because what you are is a combination of what already has been, that part is not new. When you start to live from that place, that's what's new. It might sound like the same thing to you, but to us, it's quite different.

Are there other galactic races who have these combinations? Whether it's 12 or whether it's just two or six or something like that?

Absolutely, yes. This is Raphael. There are combinations six, seven, 12, in other galaxies. Not here on Earth. We don't think you would be likely to interact with one of these multidimensional beings in your life here on Earth. Yes, other expressions of combining galactic races in this way do exist in the universe.

We would say that if you meet a being that comes in a spacecraft or other vehicle, they are likely to be a pure genetic line. The interracial intermixing is more rare in a galactic sense. Many species are just not compatible for that, in a strictly we could call it biological or energetic sense. It's not necessarily so much about hatred or war as incompatibility. This human expression is quite designed—had to overcome some of those functional frequency challenges.

. . .

Does that suggest, then, that the configuration of the 12 that were chosen of the strands to give to the New Human were ordained or deliberately chosen to match the needs of the current changes that need to happen on planet Earth?

This is Angel Raphael. Yes and not yes. The New Human was designed to ascend. It's an ascension vehicle. Because you're coming out of a one-dimensional space, for example, living in only third dimension, to multidimensionality. That created a new vehicle for that, new human vehicle for that. This planet was designed to hold this expression of ascension.

Paradoxically, or wonderfully, some other energies come in to make it the right time for that ascension. We can't answer your question in the way of linear time and prophecy. We don't see that when the 12 dimensions, these different galactic races, were chosen to combine into the human self, that there was a knowledge of this particular combination of polar shifts and solar flares and so on.

But the human is designed to ascend, so it was going to make use of some sort of energies to have the timing be right to shift into ascension mode, which you're in now.

Was the combination selected with the intention of transcending any constraints within the galaxy, of gifting to humanity the possibility of assisting the whole—or those parts of the galaxy that want to be in oneness—to go to another level?

Absolutely. This is Angel Raphael. That is 100% the intent of the design of the New Human. Some of you feel this icky feeling about: "What do you mean design?" It sounds a little non-biological. It could feel a little creepy, perhaps.

But when you look further to what is the intent of that design, it is a global harmony. It is: How do we evolve out of warfare? How do we create new insight?

Because there was this sense of being a bit stuck, having evolved as far as we can evolve. How can we take this even further? Consciousness loves to evolve and find new ways of expression.

Yes, that's a beautiful way of saying it. It was a quest for galactic understanding in a time of war. Humans were created in a time of war for the quest for something else, something different.

When we say that humans have a lot to share, we do mean that in a galactic sense. Not just person to person or human to galactic being who's visiting. This is a showcase for galactic change, absolutely. We do expect it to inform galactic events, not just human ones and not just Earth ones.

25
ACTIVATIONS AND CRYSTALLIZATIONS

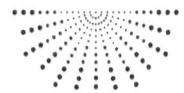

This is Angel Raphael. Activation is an important topic because people feel it should be like a light switch going on if there was nothing before, you should be able to see everything all bright, all at once, and also be able to interpret what you see. Sometimes it happens that way, most often not.

Instead, we would say an activation is more like turning on the power to the whole house and then everything's available to you, the dishwasher, the different lights, the ceiling fan and so on. Maybe you don't know what those things are yet.

An activation opens up conduits and pathways that you may not utilize right away, but it's more complete than just flipping a switch that could then be turned off. It means there is a hum, a subtle vibration, which is always active now within you, that you have access to for your own delight—your own soul mission, your own ways of being in the world, your own ways of learning.

You come out of this process of 12-dimensional activation, ready for light. The use of light is up to you. How do you use those conduits of light?

We would suggest to keep your focus, please, on the practical, the ordinary, the everyday, in addition to, of course, the extraordinary things—changes you want to see on the globe, for the environment, for society, for your enlightenment journey, whatever is important to you. It doesn't have to be all of those things in this life.

In addition to the grand scale of things, if you focus on everyday life and what do you want to see play out there, and play with these activated lines in that place of you, it begins to what we would call crystallize. Which means not harden and calcify, but shine bright and have sharp edges, the way that a gemstone has facets has sharp edges —which means it can be used as a tool. And it can be used to perceive from various vantage points, refract light and so on.

The crystallization after the activation is a way of beaming light, let's say, to oversimplify, to not be too technical. The way that a prism catches light in certain ways and can use and be a conduit for light in certain ways.

It's not that you become hard. Let the mind just be soft about what crystallization might mean. Essentially, it's when light goes fractal. First you have the activated hum, and then you build on that. Although the energy is still fluid, you build on that through the crystallization of you. That is the interdimensional aspect of all of this.

The mind doesn't have to follow that. We're just giving an overview, because many people, when they heard the word crystallize or crystalline being, they think that people will turn translucent or it means that we look like quartz crystal. It's not that.

If you watch light move through a prism, leaded glass or quartz crystal, something like that, you can see how the light can dance and form rainbows and move. If you look through the different facets or natural sides of a crystal or a mirror ball sort of shape of leaded glass, you see something different each place you look.

Even within each of the 12, let's say dragon on its own, there are many ways and viewpoints of being a dragon. This crystallization, the fractal nature of the codification of you into light—moving light, liquid light, translucent light—is multidimensional within each strand. As well as, by its nature, multidimensional, since some of these 12 strands reside in or feel most at home in other dimensions than your own. You get the multidimensionality in many ways here.

It begins to feel more and more nuanced. The way a forest is not simply trees. When you let your eyes adjust, you start to see the many layers, and some, of course, are unseen. But even with eyesight, you can see the little fungus steps up the side of the tree and mushrooms and moss under the tree and other types of plants and the animal life. Like that, the 12-dimensional activation, it never is simple, because there are 12 very different beings. Even within that, it's not just a forest made up of trees.

It's very, very nuanced and rich and deep. In the rest of this lifetime, you could continue to explore and maybe not see everything that's there. And that is right. In the same way that in one lifetime as a *Homo sapiens* human, you wouldn't expect to experience everything life has to offer—being short and being tall, for example.

You might get quite a vast range of the flavor of life in one lifetime. Of course, experience both sorrow and joy, birth and death, all of that. But really, if you look at the whole human experience, what you experience in this life is somewhat narrow, quite narrow. It's defined. It's not: "I'll just have every type of experience and every type of personality, every type of response to these different experiences." You have lived within a certain bandwidth, and that's shifted and changed as your vibrational frequency uplifts.

You don't expect of yourself to experience everything. Because you don't want to. That's the simple reason. Most people don't want to be a race car driver and a ballerina and an artist and an intellectual. Maybe three of those. You do have different variety of experience in this life, but not everything.

Similarly, the activation and the crystallization of the 12 dimensions of you doesn't mean that you are going to experience everything that's possible within dragon DNA, and everything that's possible within giant DNA, and everything that's possible within Andromedan DNA, and then also every possible combination. And every fractal combination, because there are multidimensional codifications going on.

The mind doesn't have to understand all of this language, just jargon for a moment, but it's helpful to some. So we'll leave it in there for today, these different words to say that you've changed.

Many of you by this point are active in all 12. You may identify with those later on as you become familiar with which sensation is mapped to which type of DNA strand. Because it's not important to have that map in order for those to be activated in you, it's been going on with solar light and so on, quite organically within yourself.

With these angelic activations that enhances and speeds up the process as well. You don't have to have the map in order to be active in all the 12, but over time, you're going to start to see similarities and patterns and viewpoints and be able to name and point to: "That's this one. That's Pleiadian."

But you don't need to. If you don't want to know, or you find it too confusing to figure it out, you can still have access to those gifts without naming them. Similar to how in terms of your genetic lineage here on Earth, *Homo sapiens* lineage, you might have had a great grandmother who was a baker, and you never knew that, and yet you love to bake. There are things in you that come in through your DNA, whether or not the mind knows about it. Or if you're adopted, then you really don't know, you don't have access to that information, and yet you still have strong leanings which likely do come down through the genetic line.

Similarly, when these galactic strains are active in you, you may have new joys, new delights, new repulses. Things that used to be delight you. You think: "Why would anyone want to do that?" Slightly different reactions to the world. And your range of experience will widen naturally, because you're curious about more things. You have insight into more things now. This happens naturally.

We don't want you to stress out, to try to feel: "I need to identify it with the mind." For those of you who are curious, you can research as much as you like, or do scientific experiments with yourself— meaning exercises like we've been doing over the last several months here to play out: "What is it like to walk, literally walk in the shoes of this DNA? What does it feel like, physically? What do I see or smell differently? How can the resources of that DNA help me in this scenario?" Either to be more creative, to be more intellectually in tune with what's needed, to be more empathic, to be more telepathic, and so on.

To someone from the outside, you don't look like you just grew scales and your feet got very large, that you have hallmarks of these different DNA in a physical sense that could be measured with the visual eye. However, you will start to behave new. Be more resilient. Cellular structure regenerates more easily, readily. In a way that perhaps others can notice or not, you can use those resources.

For example, the stability of dragon, or the telepathy of many of these 12, can't really be seen from the outside. But those who know you might say: "Wow, you're more sure-footed now." Or: "Wow, you have that bravery to speak in public. You never had that before. Where did that come from?" "I don't know. It just seems easy now." So you don't have to know. Very, very similar to how you don't have to know your own *Homo sapiens* genetic line.

"Where did this come from? Why do I love to play music?" Or: "Why is it accessible to me to hear music in a certain way that others cannot? Or see these bright colors. Or envision a canvas. Or taste different flavors and food combinations."

You can just enjoy that more sensory experience opens now. It's not about closing your eyes and disappearing from the world into some intangible other dimension. It is about tasting and smelling and seeing the world you are in, in different and new ways, more nuanced.

Like the forest, so many layers to see there. Once you calm down and just look around. If you're rushing through, or you think someone's chasing you, maybe you just notice the trees. At first, as things are active, you may just see the broad brushstrokes. That's fine. But we want you to know there's more.

Give it time and space, please, for you essentially to come more into the stillness of your being, to notice these things. They happen more in being than doing, although the examples we've been giving are more about doing. It's just simpler to explain that way. The essence of these 12 you will feel the most in being and not doing. The subtlety comes through that way. Sitting in quiet, you have more chance to observe these things in yourself.

DISCOMFORT

This is Angel Ariel. Change provokes discomfort in most beings—whether it is physical, emotional, intellectual, spiritual, or all of the above. The activation of 12 new galactic lines of energy provokes quite a lot of change. Through this process, there may be discomfort at times. That is to be expected.

You're not doing it wrong, if you feel a little bit like growing pains. Remember, or if some of you have children, you might have seen it, remember it more in them, how much the joints hurt when the bones were growing. There may be physical pains as you adjust to this new DNA. That is to be expected.

Watch to see: "Is this an intermittent pain? Is it flowing through? Does it seem to change day to day?" Then it's probably not something you need to rush to your doctor about. If you get stuck somewhere: "Okay, maybe it's not that. Maybe it's not the galactic DNA." Maybe it is something in your physical self that wants attention. But especially if you run all the tests and diagnostics and nothing shows up but you still feel off, maybe what you're feeling is the newness, the difference, the differentiation of what it's like to be active in a different way in your cellular you.

Some discomfort during the change is to be expected. But when you are utilizing your active self—let's say when you're "full grown"—it doesn't hurt anymore. It doesn't feel that sense of discomfort.

You still may have many years of exploration of what to do with that, similar to when your human self, *Homo sapiens*, finished growing—24 years old, more or less—the brain and all the body parts finished growing, you still continued to figure out what to do with that—with those longer legs, the brain pathways. And you're still figuring that out now. So it doesn't stop, the exploration doesn't stop. But the growing pains part does stop. If you're having that discomfort, please know that it will pass.

ALL OF THE 12

This is Angel Raphael. We'll speak now about some more of the 12 that we have not mentioned yet. Again, we touch on these very lightly, because it's in you to know who and what these are to you. Not someone else's list of qualities.

Pleiadian, we had mentioned. Lyran, Andromedan, Arcturian, Sirian —those are the ones that are perhaps most familiar to you as beings that come from other planets. Although it's here in you now.

Dragon and angel, we have discussed in the past with you. Giant, which is a very Earth being. At least you're familiar with giants on Earth, even if you thought they were fantasy.

Aboriginal Australian we have not spoken of yet. This is a very pure genetic line that still exists today as an active populace on planet Earth. And not just in that region of the world. It was in other places, and still is. But we'll use that nametag for now, because for most people, they know what that is. If you're aware, as an anthropological viewpoint, that there are other tribes that are related, yes, we see that as well. You have that in your galactic DNA, Aboriginal Australian.

Zoroastrian is one we have not yet discussed. This is another genetic line which has remained more or less quite pure—still exists today. One of the oldest "religions." You can research that if you like. That populace still exists today. You share that galactic lineage as well.

Some of these, as you have seen now, have also been distinct—like Zoroastrian and giant—"purebred," we could call them, galactic races, which existed and still do still exist here on the planet. You have that as one of your 12 strands. Again, it's a mix and a synthesis in you.

Tara is the name we will give to another one of the 12 strands. Some of you are aware of Tara as iconography in Buddhism and Hinduism. To us, this is a type of being, a Tara. People in different parts of the world saw them and created some mythology about them.

Taras do exist, male and female. Although in most of the stories, they show up as female. It is a living race on Earth which still exists. They are very, very private. Like the yeti, sasquatch, you don't see them very much, but even less so. But they have been seen. They do still exist in remote places on Earth, the Tara beings.

Very, very benevolent, the Tara beings. You will see many stories of benevolence. When a village or a person encountered Tara, it was to come help, always. Beautiful, beautiful hearts. You carry the large heart of Tara. Beautiful, compassionate heart that holds the world.

If ever now you feel: "I need some more compassion. I need some more love for this circumstance or particular person or creature in front of me," you can just intuitively ask yourself: "Okay, I want to tug on that Tara genetic line now, because I have that in me."

Reptilian we had mentioned early on, because that is one that there may be some shame or grief about. Again, there is a strength to having the thick skin and the ability to respond and react very quickly.

NOT STUCK IN HISTORY

As you have seen with Pleiadian, any of these race histories show the evolution. You are not stuck with the galactic lineage in a stuck place, historically speaking—one thing negative or positive you might know about the historical aspects of where these people have resided, or what they have done or not done. You're not stuck with any of that. Again, remember, it's a synthesis.

The New Human, what we're calling the New Human—(others will give it fancy names, for now we'll keep it simple)—the New Human is all 12 strands active, and then the crystallization, the fractalization of that. Which means you are living it into the world multidimensionally. It's not about escape and meditation. It's a lived expression in you.

You are not held to anything—your concept or anyone else's concept —of what these beings can do or will do. Maybe people have the impression of dragons: Once upon a time, many stories show dragons as warring, a warring populace. From our vantage point, that's not necessarily correct. Any more than you could say *Homo sapiens* are a warring populace. Well, yes, they do have wars. But why?

What would provoke a dragon into battle/combat? They are very protective. Again, you may want to use that—the sharp claws of you. (Again, genetically speaking, not physically. You're not going to grow claws.) You may want to use those aspects. But maybe not often, or not at all. They just are there, available.

When you get the crayon box, it has the color black. Maybe you never like black or brown or green. You never use that color. Great. Maybe you want to use black to just outline a nice bright fuchsia to let it pop, let it shine more brightly. You never are required to use any of these

12. If any of them have discomfort, it's not that you want to deactivate them. You just leave the crayon in the box.

Because you don't know. One day it may have its perfect use. We would suggest, don't be frightened or ashamed of some of the qualities that you believe any of these 12 have. Just admire that in you, that you have this full spectrum of delights. And not so much the historical regrets. If you were to look at humanity, *Homo sapiens'* history, you might feel very burdened by all of that. We would suggest you look forward and not back, when you're looking at yourself as the synthesis of the 12.

It can be helpful to look to ideas or lists if you want. Or not. Or hear different channels from these different galactic beings to get a flavor of what they might be like. But in you, they might be different. Because again, you may choose to color more with that color or less. And when you combine colors—two or three or four or five colors— you get a new color. You're really not limited to what history says about any of these 12. Or what someone else says about any of these 12.

A ndromeda. Is that the Andromeda Galaxy?

This is Raphael. Andromedans are star people. Meaning they travel quite a lot. They do come initially from Andromeda Galaxy. These beings look very unique. One to the next, it would be hard to say: "Those two beings are both Andromedan." Because they are fanciful in their shapes, the way that you may have at different points in your life loved to dress up in different kinds of clothing.

It's not that they change the shape that they choose. But one to another, brother, sister, mother, father, you couldn't tell that was a family of beings. They're quite fanciful in shape.

Let's just speak generally here about what's not included. We had mentioned, for example, Orion is not included. Yet, there are star beings from that galaxy who have interacted with Earth and may continue to do so.

The 12 doesn't mean those are the only beings that are on Earth. It means those happen to be—through fate or accident or love of consciousness expanding—those happen to be the 12 galactic beings, type of galactic beings, that got together to form humankind. Of course, there were more than 12 individuals. Let's say councils and scientists who got together and said: "Let's make a new humankind."

For better or worse, some are not included. Some of you may feel very akin to the Mantis beings or some other being. It does not mean that you did not have a past life as a Mantis being, or you don't have a present guru or guide who's a Mantis being.

These 12 doesn't limit the beings that may land in a spaceship in your yard, or that you may have a meditation or dream about, or have a remembrance.

Lemurian is also not included in these 12, and yet many of you have that remembrance of that lifetime. It does not mean that these are the only wise and beautiful 12 galactic beings. Or the best 12 galactic beings. They are marvelous. And the combination in you, from an angelic perspective, is marvelous.

However, it does not mean these are the only beings you would ever have resonance with. Some of you came in with energy from other lifetimes, or a hybridization. That's something else. We're just speaking about the activation of the New Human. It is these 12. Doesn't mean the best 12. We're not saying it as a judgment; just a factual thing.

I *would like to know a little bit more of the qualities of the Australian Aboriginals and Zoroastrian.*

This was Raphael. Zoroastrian: very, very masterful with the elements. Fire, water, earth, and there are more in that system, more elements than the ones you have grown up with. You might learn those subtle elements as well. In modern fantasy novel language, those would be the elemental magicians, you might call them. You have that in you. That's one of the qualities of Zoroastrian.

Aboriginal Australian are essentially of Earth. They are the voice of Earth. They are the people of this land. Many, many conquerors and visitors have come and gone, but these are the first people. They are the people of this Earth. And so, they sing its song better than any other race who has visited since then, or been born here since then. The life blood of the Earth is in their blood.

They will feel—and giants do as well—a volcanic movement anywhere on Earth, for example, in a physical way. Of course, that's not just that one quality, but to give you something to notice. If you start to notice in yourself a tremor, and then you hear about an earthquake somewhere, but not nearby, that might be the Aboriginal Australian in you.

T *he Taras, are they also connected to any kind of planet? Or have they also always been just on Earth?*

This is Raphael. Absolutely. They did arrive in craft, what you might call spacecraft—although not to our vision, something that we have seen in Star Trek or those kind of movies. They arrived in craft and have been on Earth since. They do have other planetary dwellings. This is, at the moment, the primary.

There are not very many of them, and they like it that way. You might think of a mountain lion. Now here we don't mean the physicality, but behavior. You would expect a mountain lion to have a wide territory and to be more or less on its own and not to want to interact with people very much. It's a little bit like that.

They love to be in the wild and on their own, more or less. Although they do interact and have babies and all of that. There is variation of color, and so on, multiple arms. All of that is from our vantage point factual.

They are remote. Sometimes, if you feel during this activation process that you suddenly want to be on your own and very far from any populace—you never have liked camping, but suddenly you want to be out on a mountaintop—that may be the Tara instinct in you.

INTERACTING WITH THE EXTERNAL 12

These different races and strands, How do they want to relate to us? I hear all about our freedom, and know that there will be variations and diversity depending on our own wishes, etc. But from their point of view, do they all want engagement from us? Or will some just be observing? Or do they have an agenda? Are they waiting for us to set the agenda?

This is Raphael. Absolutely, there is an agenda. And it's different for each of the 12.

It's been a while, also, right? It's been some decades and more, since the seeding of these dormant DNA within humankind that are now becoming awake. For the most part, the beings who started this whole thing are not alive; but they left records of some kind.

There have been those, and there are those, let's say, hovering around Earth, quite literally right now, waiting to see: how does this play out?

In Earth's predictions and history, there has been this sense of anticipation as well, around this time. Let's say the Mayan calendar— and the Mayans were not one of the 12—even they saw there's something big around this time on the planet. Or from solar or Western astrology: the Age of Aquarius. Something new is coming in now.

Many vantage points from the outside, let's say watching to see: "We heard about this." And maybe it's been so long that for some of these races, it's begun to feel like a myth. Yet, suddenly, something's happening on the Earth.

To some of these 12, it does feel very present and alive, and like scientists, they're watching to see what's going on. Not that you are under a petri dish, but they're curious.

Some have in the lineages through time, begun to think it's apocryphal, or more of a myth—something that was made up. So this may surprise some within these races as well. How does the modern brain and self interpret? The words may have been written down and passed forward, but kind of lose their meaning out of context. Now the context becomes very real.

Again, it's a lived experience. It's very real. And it's new. So it can't really be predicted. How exactly are you going to combine these 12? We do see a more empowered human, a more benign human, a more intelligent one, and one that has more abilities and nuance. We see a more interesting, more peaceful human. One of the primary reasons behind this was to create a more peaceful, powerful being.

It sounds like a ridiculous question, but who moves first? Do they expect us to take the initiative, or are they going to approach or engage us?

This is very mixed. This is Raphael. There's not a coordination here. The way you could say, let's say, politically speaking, in third dimension, there's a United Nations. Yet you wouldn't really say that for the most part, these nations, although they speak and attempt to coordinate, that they move in a coordinated way altogether. Even at the level of one nation on Earth, there's not uniformity.

You could imagine that with a certain type—let's say Andromedans— not every Andromedan is going to approach this in the same way. Certainly not every awakened human is going to approach this in the same way. It does have to do with, again, your wish. Do you want to physically see Andromedans in this life, with your eyes? (In addition to awakening to whatever that is within you.) Some people do not. And that will be honored.

This is a big, wonderful mix and muddle, case by case, person by person. In other words, purebred dragon, do they want to appear on Earth again or not? Maybe not. Maybe they'll just watch or hear about it from afar. They will feel it, that it has awakened in you. Dragons have that inner knowing.

No, there's not one script. "Here's what happens next." It's much more organic and natural than that.

I just had one day of really quite strong rage and anger recently, and knew it was part of the integration. Is there any advice the angels can give about moderating the change? Is there a particular reason that we might experience anger, or is that just something personal?

This is Raphael. In the beginning of your activation cycle, there may be some things that are clearing. Those things may be clearing the energies that were alive at the time of the first dormant DNA. If there was rage in one species or one being at that time, it clears out so that these lines can be neutral and active.

Reptilian, for example, was an unwilling and willing participant. They would have preferred, at that time, historically, that they could just have all of planet Earth for themselves, or at least two thirds. But they didn't want to be left out. So they agreed to be part of this, but it came with a lot of resentment, ill will.

As the reptilian you is activating, for many of you, that's clearing—through anger or even expressions of skin rash or acne, that kind of thing.

Some of it can be emotional clearing. Some of it quite physical. The physicality, some of the discomfort, is also calibrating to new dimensions. Some inner ear discomfort as you learn to physically hear higher vibrations, that kind of thing.

It can be both. The discomfort can be from clearing and it can be from growing pains as well. It's not important to name it: "Which thing is clearing, or is this just something in the collective?" Let's say there's rage because there was a violent event, a church shooting or something. "Maybe that's what I'm feeling today." It's not always going to be that what you feel is from the 12, but sometimes it is clearing of the line.

It's not important to really name it, know what it is. Just let it move. You can express—let it out vocally, or hit a pillow, or just let it move without needing to assign it a reason.

I have question about the difference between regeneration that happens after the activation and the growing pains. What's the switch there? And what are the hallmarks of the regeneration?

This is Rafael. The first phases of this, initially, we had said approximately seven to 10 months, once you start the activation process for the physical body to calibrate to all of this to change on the cellular DNA level, to activate all of these lines in a way that doesn't break you.

Although there may be sleepless nights and discomforts, it happens at a pace that's intelligent. The metamorphosis can happen naturally while you live your life, more or less. That is the change, the activation.

Once you are fully active and awake, then comes the exploration of these different parts of yourself. One of the different parts of yourself is you're now running a lot more energy than you used to. And you have a lot of different types of intelligence. For example, we spoke about the intelligence of Earth and also the elements. Some of those play important roles in healing. Other galactic beings are very, very fine-tuned in an intellectual sense with quantum healing.

You have access to many different types of healing now instinctually within you. The regeneration of the new cellular structure happens as soon as the transformation is complete. The youthening, essentially, of you, and longevity. Many have predicted that humans would begin to have longer life spans. New Humans do and will. The repair of what has happened to you in this life, and then a continual, rapid regeneration.

We see more health, more youthening. Not that you become young or immature, but the cells feel more pliant, viable, flexible. So greater health overall, and vitality and energy—all of that. The way that you eat may begin to change. All of that takes time. It's not going to be overnight.

First, all of these energies are doing the metamorphosis process, what we are also calling the activation. Then the crystallization is you living that in the world. Part of you living in that in the world is that you're more resourced now in terms of energy and light, what you might call voltage or frequency, and different modalities of healing. We see you being more vibrant overall, better health.

WHERE IS THIS HEADED?

All of this is in this lifetime? In the next few years we'll be able to start these explorations?

This is Adria. Because angels are not in time, I do take anything they say about time as a general guideline. Yes, I believe in this lifetime and the next few years.

This is Angel Raphael. Yes, the activation begins now, or has begun in you already. Then some of those people on the Earth who want to go through the New Human transition will start five years or seven years from now, 10 years, 12 years. It's open now. People can start when they feel ready. It has already begun for many.

Those who are born, then, in future generations come in with the 12 dimensions active. They won't have to go through this metamorphosis process. Over the next few generations, everyone becomes New Human.

It happens gradually. Not everyone who is alive right now will make that choice to become New Humans. That is respected and honored—their choice, their right to stay essentially third-dimensional *Homo sapiens* and live out the joys and challenges and learning rights and lessons from the polarity and density field there. That's still open for right now, but won't remain so.

Again, as the new generations come in and people transition (in other words, die) who didn't become 12-dimensional. Eventually, everyone on Earth will be. Everyone who is human will be New Human.

Then it's up to New Humans and *Homo sapiens* and galactic beings who are visiting or living inside the Earth to decide: Will earth become a different kind of place where there are more races coexisting? Or is it essentially going to be more or less human? Or different quadrants of the Earth?

All of that we see happening very peacefully. And it is an unknown. It can't really be predicted, because there are so many moving parts to this.

We would say within your lifetime, many, or most humans will become aware: "Galactic beings are visiting. They're peaceful," and of course, have different opinions about that. You may welcome that. Some may not. Whether or not there will be a full coexistence or just visiting is yet to be determined. It's up to you.

Some people are speaking about a return to a kind of Eden, a template for the Earth for this extraordinarily diverse, rich, highly creative environment. So maybe it's just a change of perspective. On one hand, it's an evolution, and on the other hand, it is a return to a garden of Eden type potential?

This is Raphael. In a way, yes. When humans were created, there was this playfield which was quite open so the ascension could happen, exploration could happen. It wasn't very long into this time of humans on Earth, when they were overtaken. You could say the fall from Eden, the fall from grace.

We don't mean that in the sense of the Bible story, but some of you will have a sense of what that means. We won't beleaguer that too much here. But yes, humans came out of this freedom and unlimited, and they became subject to a lot of laws which weren't really meant to be here, in terms of a negative structure influencing humankind.

Much of what is clearing in these last 7-10 years has been the dismantling of that structure of power over humankind. That's the return to: "Okay. Now let's get back to this playful unfolding. What does it mean to be human?" When humans are allowed to be unlimited and not under "power over" subjugation conditions.

The short answer is yes, it is a return. But not really like going back to a different timeline or a reset, because all of that history on Earth still exists. It is now a freedom. Angels have spoken quite a lot about freedom. That's what we mean, is now you're free to ascend and to be what you were meant to be, even though no one—none of these 12 galactic races who participated in this, or the New Humans who are awake and noticing what's going on—no one knows what this is going to be, because it's an evolution.

It's a new expression of consciousness. There's no: "This is what the New Human must be or will become." There's no prediction about "this is what it means to be the New Human."

From angelic perspective, what's important to us is that you return to that playfield of the unlimited and see what do you want to make of these 12 expressions in combination. Again, using some or all or none —up to you. But at least you have the freedom. And at most you have the freedom now to do so—to play in this abundance of unlimited.

THE 12 GALACTIC STRANDS OF DNA

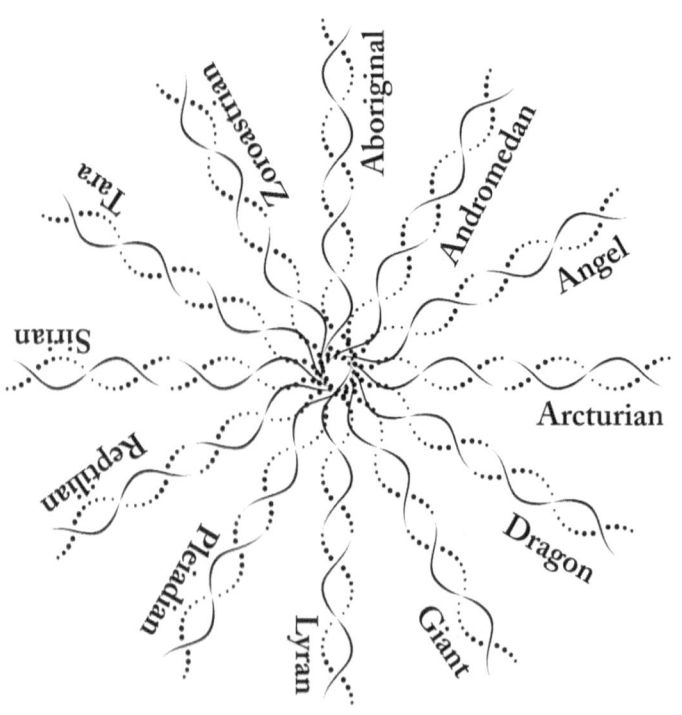

MEDITATIONS ONLINE

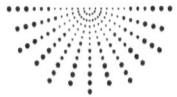

Free english-language audio of select meditations is available online at www.adriaestribou.love/12dna

Password: angelsloveme

ABOUT THE AUTHOR

 Adria Estribou is a conscious channel of angels, Lemurians, and other beings who wish to assist humanity. Along with the beings she channels, she gives you tools to thrive in the New Earth energies. Adria is also an animal communicator, sound healer, and intuitive guide.

Part 1 in this series, *Angel Insights for Unprecedented Times*, is an Amazon International Best Seller in the US, UK, Canada and Germany. Her other books include *Why Did Lemuria Fall?* and *Slip through the Keyhole*.

Adria lives in Sedona, and works with clients around the world. At the time of publication, Adria offers live weekly group angel channeling sessions and transmissions. You can find out more at www.AdriaEstribou.love and @adriaestribou on IG, Facebook and YouTube.

MORE FROM ADRIA ESTRIBOU

Books

Angel Insights for Unprecedented Times (2024)

Erkenntnisse der Engel Für Beispiellose Zeiten (2025)

Why Did Lemuria Fall? (2018)

Slip through the Keyhole (2016)

Online Courses, Transmission Recordings and Meditations

www.adriaestribou.love/shop

Live Channeling

Weekly Angel Transmissions

www.adriaestribou.love/events

Monthly Angel Transmission Subscription

www.adriaestribou.love/about-angel-transmissions-membership

REVIEWS WELCOME

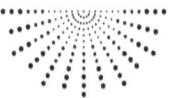

If you enjoyed this book, please post a review wherever you purchased it and/or on Goodreads.

It helps the book be found.

Thank you!